LOWELL THOMAS JR.

Flight to Adventure: Alaska and Beyond

LOWELL THOMAS JR.

with

LEW FREEDMAN

ALASKA
NORTHWEST
BOOKS®

Library of Congress Cataloging-in-Publication Data

Thomas, Lowell, 1923-
  Lowell Thomas Jr. : flight to adventure, Alaska and beyond / Lowell Thomas, Jr., Lew Freedman.
       pages cm
  Summary: "Lowell Thomas Jr. is a famed Alaskan who made his mark as a Bush pilot and by serving in state government, but who also has had a lifetime's worth of adventures that have taken him around the world. Thomas, now eighty-nine, and living in Anchorage, is the son of one of the most widely known Americans of the twentieth century, and his connection to Lowell Thomas Sr. (1892-1981) enabled him to jump-start his life of adventure at a very early age. From the time he was fifteen, Lowell Thomas Jr. has been involved in a series of journeys that have seen him cross paths with many famous lives and take part in many historic events"— Provided by publisher.
  Includes bibliographical references and index.
  ISBN 978-1-941821-63-3 (softbound)
  ISBN 978-0-88240-914-6 (hardback)
  ISBN 978-0-88240-983-2 (e-book)

  1. Thomas, Lowell, 1923- 2. Explorers—Alaska—Biography. 3. Air pilots—Alaska—Biography. I. Freedman, Lew. II. Title.
  G226.T46A3 2013
  629.13092—dc23
  [B]
                                  2013021588

Design by Vicki Knapton

Published by Alaska Northwest Books®
An imprint of

GRAPHIC ARTS
BOOKS®

P.O. Box 56118
Portland, Oregon 97238-6118
503-254-5591
www.graphicartsbooks.com

To my partner in adventure,
my wife, Tay, who passed on to her
next adventures on October 17, 2014.
And to my fellow adventurers.

—Lowell Thomas Jr.

CONTENTS

About the Authors

LOWELL THOMAS JR. has led a life of adventure, traveling around the world. Since 1960 he has been based in Anchorage, Alaska, where he and his wife, Tay, raised their family.

An author, filmmaker, and devoted small-plane pilot for about sixty-five years, and one who has on his resume approximately 1.2 million miles of flight time at the controls. Thomas is a passionate conservationist and has been honored for his work in preserving the Alaska wilderness.

LEW FREEDMAN is a longtime journalist and former sports editor of the *Anchorage Daily News* in Alaska, where he lived for seventeen years. The author of nearly sixty books, Freedman has won more than 250 journalism awards.

He and his wife, Debra, live in Indiana.

Introduction

Ifirst met Lowell Thomas Jr. when he had just completed one of his adventurous missions. He flew Alaskan mountaineer Vernon Tejas back and forth from Anchorage to Mount McKinley in 1988 as Tejas became the first climber to complete a solo winter ascent of North America's tallest mountain.

Over the last twenty-five years Lowell and I spoke periodically, worked on newspaper stories together periodically, and occasionally just talked. More than once in recent years he spoke of plans to write his memoirs. Off and on over time I asked him how it was coming, expressed enthusiasm for the idea, and said I looked forward to reading them. More recently, as he described his progress, he asked me to join him in the project and collaborate.

I was thrilled to do so because I knew Lowell's life was a great story to tell. As it turned out his story was so great, so adventurous, so much fun, that I didn't even know the half of it when we began meeting in his Anchorage home to tape-record his memories.

As he approached his ninetieth birthday, Lowell had been a small-plane pilot for more than sixty years with more than one million miles in his log. He had been an adventurer, an avid skier, photographer, film advance man, world traveler, legislator, and lieutenant governor of the state of Alaska. He was one of those men who had been everywhere, it seemed, and had flown himself to most of those everywheres in his own plane, to boot.

Among Lowell's grand adventures (beyond investigating nearly every part of Alaska), was visiting the Dalai Lama in Tibet with his father, the famed broadcaster Lowell Thomas Sr., before China overran that country. He gave a Pygmy chief his first ride in a plane. And he traveled with nomads in the desert of Afghanistan. Lowell was also the chronicler of the pioneer jet airplane flight between the North Pole and South Pole.

Sometimes Lowell, who served in the Air Corps during World War II and learned how to fly while in the military, traveled on his own. Sometimes he was in partnership with his father, Lowell Sr., and sometimes he journeyed with Tay.

The vast majority of the material contained in this autobiography of Lowell Thomas Jr. was taken from lengthy tape-recorded interviews of his recollections made during 2012. In addition, a small amount of material was included from prior interviews done over the years.

Some material was also compiled separately by Lowell Thomas Jr. in diary form and taken from these unpublished writings as he initially had prepared to write this book on his own. Other material was taken from reports he made in books chronicling his earlier life adventures. In some instances, wife Tay Thomas contributed recollections from the adventures and journeys she shared with her husband. Lowell Thomas Sr. passed away in 1981. However, he was a prolific writer and in some cases his published work touched on some of the adventures he shared with his son.

Two books written by Lowell Thomas Jr. that were consulted were *Out of This World: Across the Himalayas to Forbidden Tibet* and *The Dalai Lama: A Biography of the Exiled Leader of Tibet*. One book cowritten by Lowell Thomas Jr. and Tay Thomas consulted was *Our Flight to Adventure*. One book cowritten by Lowell Thomas Jr. and Lowell Thomas Sr. consulted was *Famous First Flights That Changed History: Sixteen Dramatic Adventures*. Books written by Lowell Thomas Sr. consulted were

Good Evening Everybody: From Cripple Creek to Samarkand and *So Long Until Tomorrow: From Quaker Hill to Kathmandu*.

Each chapter in this book contains some introductory material that presents the context of the times, the people Lowell Jr. was interacting with, or the background for the trip or adventure in that portion of his life. Then follows Lowell's own account of what happened during the course of the event, sometimes with observations from Tay, or his father Lowell Sr., interspersed.

To some degree Lowell Thomas Jr. has led two completely different lives. He has resided in Alaska for more than fifty years, but he was involved in so many amazing trips before even moving to the state that the list would make even members of The Explorers Club jealous.

Even those who know Lowell from his decades in Alaska will probably be surprised to learn of some of his earlier-in-life adventures. One reason is that he is a soft-spoken man, not prone to brag. Whether anyone would label the recounting of many of Lowell's life's experiences as boasting here, it should just be noted that he is telling it like it was.

Lowell was only sixteen when he first visited Alaska on a mountain climbing trip and he fell in love with the territory, its beauty and vastness. About seventeen years passed before he returned and after that, when Alaska became a new state, Lowell and Tay decided this last frontier seemed like a very inviting place to raise a family. Alaska has been home since 1960.

While most of his time spent in Alaska has been very pleasurable, one of the most disconcerting experiences Lowell and his family ever endured was living through the 9.2 magnitude 1964 Great Alaska Earthquake and losing their home to the second-most powerful quake in world history.

While the vast majority of his time spent in the air was joyful, since Lowell was doing something he loved, one can't spend more than 10,000 hours in flight, much of it flying over rugged countryside in a part of the world known for its powerful weather elements, without the occasional mishap. By the time Lowell retired from flying at age eighty-six, he had had his share. But one of his prouder achievements was never cracking up a plane that couldn't be readily repaired. Somehow Lowell and his airplane always made it home.

From the first moment Lowell spent time in Alaska in 1940, through the present, he has never tired of admiring the rugged beauty of the land. Through use of his airplane, and his ability to fly it to all corners of the state, sometimes for fun, sometimes for rescues, sometimes merely to transport sightseers, he has been able to explore far more of the forty-ninth state than most Alaskans. Alaska has 586,000 square miles and sometimes it seems as if Lowell has seen them all from overhead.

—Lew Freedman

1

Flight to Adventure

Adventure was bred into Lowell Thomas Jr.'s soul and was clearly part of his makeup from an early age. The desire and need to travel and explore new worlds was as natural a part of his existence as walking, talking, eating, or sleeping. Thomas was raised in a family that thrived on adventure, and on travel in the United States and around the world. It rubbed off on him. His father, Lowell Thomas Sr., was the foremost adventure traveler of his day, an intrepid journalist who crisscrossed the world to explore and to report.

Young Lowell took after his dad from an early age. Partially through his own desire and partially through his father's influence, even as a teenager Thomas was able to broaden his mind by taking unusual trips not available to his classmates. The interest piqued at a young age never waned, particularly if it involved flying somewhere new. By the time he was a young man Thomas was fully smitten by aviation possibilities and there was nothing he enjoyed more than taking the controls and transporting himself from Point A to Point B in his own airplane.

It was natural too, that when searching for a partner, Lowell Thomas Jr. would seek out someone like-minded, someone who embraced the thrill of visiting places that were off the beaten track. In 1948, Lowell found someone who was equally at home in the air and equally as enthusiastic about seeing the world. Tay Pryor was the daughter of one of his father's friends, a commercial airline executive. She made a logical and endearing match for Lowell Thomas Jr. Once married they embarked on a journey that would serve as one of the most remarkable and daring honeymoons perhaps in all of American history.

Beginning with the planning in 1953, the Thomases' life of marriage and adventure began together in a way that almost no marriage had ever begun before. It was up, up, and away, to parts unknown. They decided to fly around the world in a small airplane, with Lowell piloting, Tay navigating, and the unknown passing beneath their wings. They traveled on their own schedule, they traveled where tourists never traveled at all, and they had no time limit. Truly, the sky was the limit.

The flight began in March of 1954 in Paris with Lowell at the controls of a Cessna 180 that was nicknamed *Charlie*. One civilization, one group of people inhabiting a different kind of world that Lowell and Tay Thomas hoped to visit with during their sojourn were Pygmies.

They got their chance in the Congo, where the Bambuti Pygmies live in small groups. They reside in a tropical rain forest and in the 2000s it is estimated that between thirty thousand and forty thousand members of the tribe still exist. Even today they remain primarily hunter-gatherers and the primary produce in their diet is gleaned from the land: yams, berries, fruits, leaves, and nuts. Decades after the Thomases' visit with the Pygmies the group still hunts for the meat they eat with bow and arrow and nets, not firearms.

❖ ❖ ❖

LOWELL: The leader of the Pygmies was Faisi and he proved he was the bravest of his tribe by taking a ride with me.

We were in the Congo. We had heard of a woman named Anne Putnam. I believe the Belgian administrator at Mambasa told us the best way to see the Pygmies was to go to Camp Putnam. She and her husband, Patrick, [who died a few months before the visit] lived among the Pygmies. She wrote a book about living among them. We wanted to look her up. There is an image of the Congo as all jungle and it was a jungle at the time.

Navigating over the Congo was a real challenge for both of us because we had to follow one road, a dirt road, that wound through the jungle and we really had to watch carefully to make sure it wouldn't disappear under us. We were looking for an airstrip, a small airfield that had been built by the Belgian airline Sabena. It was carved out of the jungle. I wasn't sure if it was just used for emergencies or not, but it was a grass field and we heard about it.

You have to realize that in the early 1950s there was no tourism in places like the Congo and many of the other places we visited. We wanted to see people who lived in the remotest part of the world and who still lived the way they had for many years. We had to get clearance from our State Department to make the trip. We had paperwork for everywhere we wanted to go, so when we reached each country they would let us in and let us stay. Still, there seemed to be many suspicions about what we were doing there. Nobody came to visit the places we wanted to go and some local authorities figured we must have been up to something. Most places, as soon as Tay and I got there, we were welcomed and they were glad to have us—but not always.

We found our landing field, but it was a two-hour truck ride on a one-lane dirt road from Camp Putnam. We were lucky enough to hitch a ride through the forest with a young Belgian agricultural expert. After a while we saw a sign that read, "Camp Putnam. Meals. Lodging" at the edge of a forest. It was now pouring rain. We passed a tiny village that consisted only of a small cluster of huts and a handful of natives who watched us silently as we passed.

There is a kind of code of the wilderness of being hospitable when you live in the middle of nowhere. Alaskans abide by it, as well. Not many people are going to show up in remote areas and although Anne Putnam wasn't expecting us, it wasn't as if she had company or customers very often. If we were going to visit with the Bambuti

Pygmies this was the way to do it, through Anne Putnam. There were no translators with us. They didn't speak English and we didn't speak their language.

So we showed up at Anne Putnam's large, attractive, thatched-roof house. We were utterly unprepared to find a band of Pygmies usurping the hearth in Anne Putnam's living room. It was no wonder they were huddling around the fire, for with the rain falling steadily there was no real warmth in the air. In the hot African climate they wore bark loincloths and were bare-chested. The children under five wore nothing at all. We learned right away that we were going to have to converse in sign language.

TAY: It was so interesting because her home was open to the Pygmies and they would just come and go and make themselves at home and that became our temporary home too. We had always heard that these people were very shy and they were, but they were very close to her and you could tell. Mrs. Putnam spoke to them in their language, which was Swahili. Some two hundred little people of this area accepted Anne Putnam as their "Big Chief." The first night we ate with her and the Pygmies at a very long table that served as her dining room. The room had a straw roof, but it was open on the sides. Pygmies slowly and quietly gathered around the table. I don't remember exactly what we ate, but there was rice and we had a big bowl of soup. All of a sudden this large spider dropped down from the roof into my soup with a splash. I believe I shrieked. It was a huge, hairy spider and although it was the kind of scene one only sees in the movies, it was real. I was never very happy about spiders anyway.

Our little plane was packed tight with clothing and camera gear and we were there hopefully to make a documentary. After some time passed Anne asked us, "Would you like to go into the forest with the Pygmies and do some filming of their home life? They will make you a little house." It was exciting to be with them even if we couldn't communicate in anything except basic sign language. In size and behavior, they were like little children. They came up to our shoulders in height.

LOWELL: The Pygmies formed a delegation that had come to invite us to a festival, and they conveyed their invitation by prancing around and chanting in high-pitched voices to the accompaniment of a crude kind of wooden flute. To ears not yet attuned to Pygmy music it was noise rather than melody, though Tay and I, after ten days exposure to such sounds, were able to detect certain melodic passages and even occasional interesting ventures into counterpoint. We all accepted the invitation, of course.

TAY: It was just so special to be with these people in the forest. They made a little house for us out of straw and palm fronds. It had a little door and we had cots inside that belonged to Anne and she had another little house nearby. Lowell and I lay there at night as the Pygmies built a big bonfire in the middle of the clearing. They had their little huts all around it too. Then they danced around the fire and sang. It was a lot of fun to hear them during the night. They called out in their language. The next day we asked Mrs. Putnam what they were saying as this went on all night. She said they were talking to the spirits in the trees, the owls, and the other animals around us. The only problem with being there was the ants. They occasionally bit us all over.

The Pygmies seemed to be playing as they ran around us, and they also swung on vines. There was a lot of chanting.

LOWELL: By way of a grand climax to our visit among the Pygmies, we took Faisi, a leader of the Pygmies, for an airplane ride. We invited others too, but Faisi was the only one who seemed willing to accept. This went hand in hand with his reputation as the very bravest of all the Bambuti, and the only one in all that section of the forest with an elephant to his credit, an elephant he killed by slipping silently through the forest until he was able from almost beneath the animal to drive a spear into its vitals.

The government agent who was in charge of the nearby elephant training center drove us to the airstrip. A native soldier who had guarded *Charlie* had done his work well. No elephants had rubbed against it and no hyenas had tried their teeth on its tires. Tay and I took off for Irumu, half an hour away, and filled our tanks, coming back at once to the Pygmies.

Never before had I seen so much excitement over an airplane. It must have been similar to the early barnstorming days at home. Because the sun was good for filming we asked Faisi to climb in first and he did so without hesitation. At our suggestion, Anne Putnam had given him a somewhat detailed briefing, explaining as forcefully as possible that the control wheel that stood only a few inches in front of him was linked to mine and that it should be considered as though it were "a charging bull elephant—something to be left utterly alone." We got Faisi all buckled into the passenger seat and he grabbed the strap (which Anne Putnam had compared to a "tree, a place of safety") very intently. He held on very, very tight as Tay climbed into the back.

We took off and just circled around the area a little bit. He looked down and saw all his friends way down below on the ground and he said, "They're just so small." He was calm.

TAY: I was scared of what he might do sitting in the front seat. I thought he might panic, or he could have grabbed Lowell and sent us into a tailspin. I really had no idea what could happen. He didn't know anything about flying. I sat in the back holding a bottle, maybe it was a fire extinguisher, ready to hit him over the head if he panicked, but he didn't. When we got out of the plane Faisi did something that surprised us. He bent down and picked up a blade of grass and he showed it to all of the gathered Pygmies. "I think you were this big," he said.

LOWELL: The Pygmies took me on a hunt one day. They had spears and bows and arrows. There was some kind of poison on the tips so if they hit an animal it would spread and kill it. We did not see much game, but one of the main things the Pygmies had for meat was the okapi. People think of okapis as being part of the deer family and they appear to be, but they have some stripes on parts of their bodies that resemble zebras and it is said they are in the giraffe family. I don't think they are found anywhere except in the Congo.

Lowell about to give a plane ride to Faisi, the boldest member of the Congo Pygmy tribe he and Tay visited in the jungle on their 1954–55 journey.

They took me out for the experience, at least, to show me how they hunted, but I don't remember anything being harvested. While we were out in the forest, they stopped me and pointed up a tree. It had a bees' nest and honey. They were crazy about honey. It may have been the only sugar in their diet. When they located a nest they built a fire and worked to smoke the bees out. They climbed the tree—I climbed too—to go after the honey.

It was impossible to do that without getting stung. Then they ate the honey within the comb, and the dead bees, as well. Guess we would call that a local delicacy.

Meat didn't seem to be that important to them, and we heard that sometimes they traded meat for sweet potatoes.

TAY: Later, when we were touring in the USA, giving lectures and showing films, we had the tape recording of the music the Pygmies made and we played that at many colleges and universities, at Carnegie Hall in New York, and at the National Geographic Society. There were always big crowds and most of them were older people. But it was something to think of being the conduit of the culture between the Pygmies and Americans.

LOWELL: It was a little bit sad to leave the Pygmies because we knew we would never see them again. It was the kind of side trip that one never forgets, but you can't stay in one place too long when you aim to fly around the world. I remember Faisi, though, and what a special thing it was to take him flying. He probably remembered his airplane flight with me for the rest of his life too. He probably never took another one.

You have to wonder what happened to the Pygmies in that area of the Congo. So much time has passed and a war has been fought in that country. We can't really know if that group is still there. Did they modernize? Did they just blend in with the rest of the people in that country eventually?

TAY: If they have been pretty much left alone over the years, I would think they have not changed much.

Even today if we tell people that we spent time with the Pygmies in the jungle they look at us a little bit strangely. They can't believe we did that. To them it sounds as if we were part of a movie when actually we were trying to make movies.

2

Early Life

I t is appropriate that world traveler Lowell Thomas Jr., citizen of the United States of America, was not born in the United States, but in London when his father, world traveler Lowell Thomas Sr., and mother Fran, were visiting England.

That was the first indication that Thomas's life might lead him to foreign lands—he couldn't even stay home for his own birth. Due to Lowell Thomas Sr.'s career, one which kept him on the go fantastically piling up miles by any means possible at a time when commercial air travel was in its infancy, perhaps the odds did favor the likelihood of Lowell Jr.'s birth taking place beyond the borders of his home country.

Lowell Thomas Sr. was the best-known radio broadcaster in the United States and he was the first truly national broadcaster—and for a time the only one. Any American of a certain age who listened to radio news was aware of the name of Lowell Thomas. That also meant that the newsmakers were aware of him, as well. Lowell Sr. had a signature sign-on at the start of his radio program: "Good Evening, Everybody." He also had a signature sign-off: "So Long Until Tomorrow." When Lowell Sr., the author of many books, wrote his autobiography, he split it into two volumes, one titled with the same phrase as his sign-on and the other titled with the same phrase as his sign-off.

It was common for Lowell Thomas Sr. to be granted access to the corridors of power and he became quite friendly with some of the most famous and powerful leaders of his time. As such, Lowell's upbringing was affected by his father's job, hobbies, and way of life. Lowell Sr. went to a great deal of trouble and cost (he estimated that it cost him five hundred thousand dollars over the years) to broadcast from a private, remote New York state studio rather than basing himself in Manhattan. That location, in addition, played a major part in Lowell Jr.'s upbringing.

Lowell Thomas Sr. was born in 1892 in Colorado and his breakthrough as a well-known journalist occurred during World War I when he basically "discovered" Lawrence of Arabia's exploits in the desert, rode with him, and told the world about his leadership. Thomas Sr. wrote a best-selling book about Lawrence of Arabia and the notoriety attendant to his work on the subject propelled him to fame. Over the decades he lectured actively about Lawrence and by the time Lowell Jr. was a youth, Lowell Sr. was well-known in Washington, D.C. and entertained cordial enough relations with President Franklin D. Roosevelt that the sitting president journeyed to his home to coach a baseball team playing on the Thomases' grounds.

Lowell Jr. was born on October 6, 1923, in England because his parents were there for Lawrence of Arabia lectures.

❖ ❖ ❖

LOWELL: I was born in London. My father was lecturing on Lawrence. He had just written his book about being with Lawrence in Arabia, which was a huge success and really started everybody investigating Lawrence. I don't think people knew much about him until my father came out with his big, illustrated lecture.

My father and my mother, Frances Ryan, were in England for his appearances when it became apparent I was due. I almost didn't make it in my birth and my mother almost didn't make it in childbirth either.

I didn't know that for the longest time. My daughter, Anne, was going through some family letters at Marist College. Among my mother's letters she found one that she wrote to her mother in Denver saying that it was a very close call and they had to cut her a bit. I guess I was very big at birth. They had to pull me out with forceps and so forth. My mother was never able to have another child. I was an only child. She was in labor for three days. Anyway, it was a pretty close thing and a lot of kids in those circumstances back then didn't make it. Some never made it out alive. I almost didn't make it, but I'm still here.

LOWELL SR. (memoir): Obviously October 6, 1923, was a momentous day in our lives. [In Dublin, the next day] "I also wanted to let you know I am married to a wonderful girl whose family name is Ryan, and who yesterday presented me with a fine baby boy, so now the Lowell Thomases have their own little Irishman." That one brought the house down. I, of course also told how T. E. Lawrence's family had come from Ireland.

Just after Christmas (we) boarded the venerable White Star liner *Adriatic* and set sail for home, at long last. For a while it looked as though we wouldn't make it. In mid-Atlantic we ran into the terrific winter storm of 1924 and for two days we lay hove-to, the ship rolling up on her beams and the decks awash. I quit counting my sea voyages after a hundred, but this one was easily the wildest. Blinding sheets of rain whipped by seventy-five-mile-per-hour winds turned the world into a gray maelstrom. Dishes, chairs, passengers—whatever wasn't tied down—went crashing into the nearest bulkhead. No one slept, except Lowell, twelve weeks old, happy as a clam in his laundry basket, securely wedged into a corner. Finally, the winds subsided and we came limping into New York Harbor. The lady with the torch was a welcome sight.

LOWELL: The first several weeks of my life—not that I remember them—were spent in England. Then we came across the Atlantic Ocean on an ocean liner. At that time my family was settled somewhere on Long Island and that's where we were for a little while. Then my father managed to buy a farm in Dutchess County, New York, near Pawling, on Quaker Hill. Pawling was not very big and even now all it has is about eight thousand people.

It was a dairy farm and I spent my earliest years on the farm with family. When I got to be about eleven, I started working with the cows. I helped with the haying and mowing and things like that, running the horses. That seems like a very long time ago. It seems like another life-time. It's almost eighty years back now, way back. It was a great place to grow up. It was a very rural, quiet country with forested hills. The winters were great. We had enough snow to go out and learn to tobog-gan and to ski a little bit.

We spent a lot of time right there on the farm. But my father did a lot of traveling to gather material for his lectures and his books. He published fifty-five books over his lifetime. He did one on India and one on Afghanistan. When he went off to do that research my mother went with him. I was only about two years old when they dropped me off at another farm, Locust Farm, it was called, about twenty miles away. It was run by three elderly sisters and none of them were mar-ried. It was sort of a foster home for me. My parents left me there for a long time and I still have memories of that, how I felt. It was a pretty sad time for me to be left behind.

I was left behind for months, almost a year. That happened a few times when I was little, up until the time I started grade school. My mother gave me a start in some kind of nursery school and shortly after I got old enough to start grade school my father got into radio, about 1930, and we moved to New York City for a while. We had a suite at the Waldorf Astoria Hotel. We lived in one of those tall towers. We stayed there during the winter, but in the summer, when there was no school, my mother and I would go back to the farm. My father spent quite a bit of time commuting. It was too long a trip, either by car or rail then to go back and forth to New York City to do his broadcast. Now it takes about an hour and a half, depending on traffic.

That's the way it went for a while. I went to a private school called the Lawrence Smith School in New York and I can still recall walking from the Waldorf up Lexington Avenue to Seventieth Street. The school was located between Lexington Avenue and Third Avenue. I went to school there until I reached high school age. I ended up going to prep school, The Taft School, in Watertown, Connecticut.

I never liked New York City. I did not like New York City at all, the big city. For years, roughly between 1932 and 1938, while I was going to school there, boys of school age had to go to something called the Knickerbocker Greys. The Greys were attached to the US Army Seventh Regiment and we had to learn to march and to salute and carry rifles, do close order drill, that kind of thing. Twice a week I would go to this Knickerbocker Greys thing and the purpose was to learn how to get along with other people and to develop some ability to be disciplined. It was a pretty good experience.

The only other thing I did in New York while I lived there that had any meaning for me was going to dancing school, learning how to dance. I did have rhythm. I was a pretty good dancer, but not anymore at my age. I was pretty good. They taught us the fox trot, the waltz, the basics. I did that between the ages of about eight and twelve.

Those were my early days in New York, but on the weekends we left New York and went up to the country to the farm, and then it was back down again late on Sunday, back to the city.

While I was going to school, my father was on the radio. He would come on the air every day, Monday through Friday, at quarter to seven in the evening. He became the most outstanding newsman of the time. It was NBC first, as I recall. The call letters were WJZ.

And then he got to be the news commentator for Fox Movietone News. They had a place in New York on the West Side and two nights a week he would spend until two or three o'clock in the morning editing the film and doing the commentary. The news film came in from all over the world. They showed the news films in movie theaters and my father was the voice behind the news.

For those people too young to remember—and before they had the six o'clock news on TV—when you went to the movies in those days they ran shorts before the feature. You had a cartoon, maybe a little travel segment, then they had the news, and the feature came on. So my father was very prominent in that. It kept him awfully busy. This meant that everyone knew his name. If you saw the newsreel and knew the voice and the name, every time you went to the movies you got this guy named Lowell Thomas.

His nickname was Sonny for a long time. Everyone knew him. I would go out in the streets with my father and was anxious to get to Madison Square Garden or wherever we were going, and people would stop him to talk. I'd get very upset because my dad would stop and chat with these people that wanted to meet him. It was kind of a pain in the neck for a kid, for me. I wanted to spend the time with him.

When I was young I didn't really share vacations with my father. We didn't work on any projects together either. He did start helping me to learn how to be a film commentator, a lecturer, putting together illustrated lectures by the time I was in high school. He taught me how to use a movie camera. He had some of the earliest 16-millimeter cameras, so he got me started with that. What I learned to observe helped me with my diary. He was a very good coach, very helpful. It really was a close relationship, even if I did have to share him, which bothered me when I was young.

One thing that was very intriguing for me, and something I told Tay about, was how my father used to have so many interesting people come to the house when I was a kid. He was always busy writing and telling stories about people who'd done great things. They would come over to the house in Pawling. Jimmy Doolittle was a fairly frequent visitor. Doolittle was one of the most famous pilots in the country between World War I and World War II and he won the Congressional Medal of Honor in World War II.

They always came to the country, not to see us in New York. There was a very famous German sea captain named Felix von Luckner, who after World War I came to the United States. He had a remarkable life and my father wrote a book about him called *Count Luckner: The Sea Devil* in 1927. He had been a raider for the Germans during World War

I and he was a very romantic kind of a fellow. What he somehow did was capture other ships without there being any casualties on either side. During World War II he was harassed by the Nazis, but survived a death sentence and moved to Sweden after that war. Felix von Luckner came and spent quite a bit of time with us on our farm while Dad was interviewing him. That was a wonderful time. It was a great experience. Von Luckner was full of humor and he had a lot of wonderful tricks. He would put things up his sleeve and ask, "Where do you think it went?" All that kind of stuff. I had a wonderful time with him.

Jimmy Doolittle made a big impact on me and so did Eddie Rickenbacker, who was a World War I ace and also won the Congressional Medal of Honor. Early on I developed an interest in aviation and knew I wanted to get into it in one way or another. It took quite a long time after meeting those heroes before I did.

I understood that my father's job was different than the jobs most other kids' fathers had. It seemed to be that he stood completely way off in a different area totally, another world. I knew that famous people like this just didn't drop by my friends' houses. One of our neighbors was the head of the *Wall Street Journal* and in later years the newsman Edward R. Murrow lived in the same community. Things were always lively at our house, but there were a lot of farm kids nearby too, and they were my closest friends. We'd get together and raise hell and get in trouble. Probably from the time I was ten we used to go out and chase down cats, fire air rifles at windows in the barns. One of the guys was a little bit older and he had a Model A Ford. We took turns driving it, even though we weren't old enough, seeing how fast we could go.

My father was an avid skier and that helped make me into one. We developed our interest in skiing very early on. We got with it almost from the point it was introduced to the United States as a downhill sport. The Austrians really developed it. They made the first bindings where you could actually secure your heel to the ski and you could bend forward. We did a lot of skiing in the winter. We went to Lake Placid in New York and Stowe, Vermont, and into Canada to the Laurentian Mountains in Quebec. My father had a lot to do with the

Lowell Thomas Sr. was a famed broadcast journalist and here he is with son
Lowell Jr. at about age seven.

development of several ski areas. He put a lot of money into the Aspen resort in Colorado at one point. We went out there at least once a year to Aspen and Sun Valley. Boy, those were great times.

For me it was the fun of skiing fast and making sweeping turns, going over jumps, big jumps. It was just a wonderful sport. I loved it. It was my number one sport. Dartmouth is famous as a ski college and when I got to Dartmouth I was on the ski team. Skiing has been a lifelong interest. I did downhill and ski jumping, but not cross-country. I came to ski jumping slowly, later. I did most of my college after I got out of the Air Force and that's when I really pursued ski jumping. It's a scary thing. It really is. On that *Wide World of Sports* show they had the theme of "the thrill of victory and the agony of defeat" that everyone remembers and the agony of defeat is a ski jumper crashing. Once you start down that inrun you're committed. There's no going, "Wait, I can't do it." It's too late. You've just got to go for it and hope for the best. At the least you've got to learn how to fall. Landing is the hard part. You have to learn how to avoid falling and get up enough courage to go down the ramp. You have to start on smaller hills, but it takes a lot of guts to jump, not just up, but to jump out. Really, it's like flying. The wind on your chest and your arms keeps you from tumbling over and then when you're landing on a steep hill and come down just right it's fun. Sometimes it doesn't work properly and you take a big fall. It happened to me a few times. Once I fractured a neck bone and I had to quit jumping that year.

My father started me and my mother on skiing when I was probably seven. We never did any cross-country racing, but we did do a lot of touring, pretty much in the backcountry, not competing at all. The Norwegians, the Finns, and the Swedes, the Scandinavian countries, were the best at cross-country skiing. I never got into it for racing. I had good reason. At one point I got rheumatic fever that put me into the hospital for a while. They found a heart murmur and warned me not to overdo it. Racing would push the heart too hard, so I stayed away from cross-country competition. Doing the other skiing was fine.

Lowell Jr. loved playing baseball as a youth. This is his local team. He is in the front row, extreme right, at about eleven years old.

My other favorite sport as a kid was baseball. We had a baseball team we formed and played hardball during the summer. There was no formal baseball diamond. We laid out our own field. We paced out the distances. We got good enough that we could go play other teams at some of the summer camps nearby. There was a Boy Scout camp that wasn't far away and we played against them. We played against a village team and then against some other nearby towns. That was great. We practiced quite a bit and we got pretty good. Mostly, I was a second baseman.

I kept playing baseball throughout school. I didn't play for the college, but I kept playing baseball as long as I could. At Taft, the prep school, I played more in the outfield. I had a pretty good arm, so they put me out there. I was good at catching balls. I was a pretty good hitter, but I didn't get to pitch. I was glad to be in the outfield catching flies. I did that and played football, basketball, and ice hockey. I tried a little bit of everything. But skiing became my best sport. We didn't do much skiing at Taft in Watertown, Connecticut, that's for sure. I had to pretty much wait on my skiing until I got to Dartmouth. My best sport was baseball—I got a very early start in baseball. I wasn't quite so good in basketball.

I started following the Yankees and Giants and Dodgers. Babe Ruth had just retired. Frankie Frisch was playing second for the Giants. Lou Gehrig was still playing in those days. Mel Ott was also with the Giants in New York. I think I was a bigger fan of the Brooklyn Dodgers than either of the others, though. My dad and I used to go to the ballgames in New York quite often. I think we went to all of them, Yankee Stadium, the Polo Grounds, and Ebbets Field. Those were good days, you bet. Then Joe DiMaggio came into his prime with the Yankees.

In Pawling, we had a softball team that my father organized. It was called The Nine Old Men. One of the teams they played against every year was President Roosevelt's team. The media would come to write about it too. FDR's team would come from Washington to our farm in Dutchess County and Roosevelt would coach his team from his open motor car. It was a pretty big thing for my father. He played. He was a pretty good athlete who played in high school. I was the bat boy for some of those games with the president. That was a pretty big thrill.

LOWELL SR. (memoir): I marvel at the fun and enthusiasm those games generated, the crowds that turned out to see us play, the teams thrown together at the drop of a challenge. The luminaries, many of them highly unlikely ballplayers, who came to enliven the games— Sir Hubert Wilkins, Grantland Rice, Eddie Rickenbacker, Vilhjalmur Stefansson, Rube Goldberg, Henry Morgenthau Jr., Jimmy Doolittle, Westbrook Pegler, Jimmy Walker—and I could go on and on.

Then came the December Sunday in 1941 with the news of the Japanese attack on Pearl Harbor. A golden age was over for all of us, for all Americans. And in the spring it was poignantly underscored by a brief letter I received from President Roosevelt: "Dear Lowell, I am afraid Hitler has ended our ball games for the duration . . . . As ever yours, F.D.R."

3

First Adventure

Lowell Thomas Jr. was just fifteen years old in 1939 when he embarked on his first serious adventure. He was a high school student on summer vacation from The Taft School when Lowell Sr.'s contacts gave him entrée to a trip that would be the envy of most teenaged boys. While boys his age might spend the summer riding bicycles, hanging out at the local swimming hole, or playing baseball, Lowell received a unique opportunity, one that most surely would not be available ordinarily to anyone else who was less than twenty-one.

Lowell was fairly certain he wanted to be involved in photography, moviemaking, or something similar in the long run, though he was also much too young to lock into a career. But his experience under his father's tutelage, coupled with a natural eye for what made a good picture, enabled his dad to recommend him for a spot on a trip.

One of Lowell Thomas Sr.'s friends was a cameraman with Fox Movietone News who was going to spend a chunk of the summer filming for the United States Navy as ships made a tour of Central and South America to "show the flag" to allies. Lowell Sr. suggested that the cameraman, Bonney Powell, might need an assistant on the journey. "Hey, how about taking my son?" Lowell Sr. said. "He's fifteen years old. He's just about fully grown. He's a tough kid." Powell said he would entertain the idea, as long as the Navy signed off on the plan.

❖ ❖ ❖

LOWELL: It was the summer of 1939, which would have been after my sophomore year in high school at Taft. My father and Bonney talked about the idea of me going along on this friendship tour one night when they had a break from making the newsreels at the Movietone offices. Bonney applied to the Navy and they said, "Sure, bring him along if you want to."

I turned out to be the only civilian since even my boss was a reserve officer; the only civilian out of three heavy cruisers. On board, Bonney was Commander Powell. The ships were named the *San Francisco, the Quincy,* and the *Vincent.* There were hundreds of seamen on board the ships. I was on the USS *San Francisco.* It was the flagship. I stayed with that ship the entire time.

Luckily, I had my own bunk, right next to Commander Powell. We got along very well and I learned quite a bit about photography and cinematography from him. It was great experience, just unbelievable. Now that I look back on it, it seems almost incredible that a kid of fifteen who was not in the Navy would get to go on something like that. But it happened through connections.

One day my father came to me and broached the subject. He said, "Here's a wonderful opportunity. You're invited to go along and boy, what a chance it is for you." I said, "Yes, it sounds great to me." At that point I had some knowledge of a 16-millimeter camera. This would be doing some learning on the job, a postgraduate class, you might say. I was Bonney Powell's right-hand man, his assistant, and I shot film right alongside him. He had a contract to film for the Navy. When the trip was all over, I developed my own illustrated lecture about the cruise, South America, and the Navy. My dad, who had a lot of experience making those, helped me put that together. He gave me some coaching. It turned out to be my first illustrated lecture and it

The first great adventure of Lowell Thomas Jr.'s occurred in the summer of 1939 at age fifteen when he worked as a photographer's assistant on a US Navy cruiser to several countries in South America.

was popular. I was going around doing shows when I was just sixteen. I gave that lecture off and on during my school days and it drew pretty good crowds most everywhere.

Actually, this trip started even before summer vacation began. I had to get permission to leave school in the spring, by April for sure. They didn't give me any problem about taking the time off for a trip like that. What an education.

The journey started at Guantanamo Bay. We went to Caracas, Venezuela, and on to Montevideo, Buenos Aires, and through the Straits of Magellan. We stopped at Lima, Peru. We went through the Panama Canal.

At each of the ports of call in these nations the dignitaries of the various countries would be invited on board and the admiral of the fleet and his party would go ashore. It was waving the flag, just reminding the nations in South America that we were their friends. It seemed obvious by then that World War II was going to break out and this trip was to remind these nations to pay attention to us in North America and that we were not going to let them join up with the Axis. It was supposed to be about friendship, a goodwill cruise. That's what it was called.

I had the run of the ship and just to watch the running of the ship was very exciting, very educational. I spent quite a lot of time on the bridge or in the engine room. The admiral treated me like I was his grandson almost. When they went on shore they had the usual thing with the dignitaries, parades and things. When the higher officers went off to take care of business I went along with some of the younger officers fresh out of Annapolis and the US Naval Academy. They were the ensigns on board the *San Francisco* and they treated me like a kid brother.

Of course when Navy men went ashore it was like a vacation for them. I learned to smoke cigars and drink cerveza. I discovered beer. I did develop a taste for beer at the time even if I was significantly underage for drinking. I really saw the sights, saw the seamy side of life, though nothing really bad, as well as the frosted side. We went into red-light districts. I was underage for that too. I didn't get involved in any of the bad houses of ill repute, but of course some of the sailors did.

Aboard the USS *San Francisco* in 1939.

Some of them ended up getting thrown into prison on shore and had to be bailed out. They had too good of a time. You know how it goes when the Navy goes ashore in a foreign country. I didn't get into any trouble like that, but I had a great time, I really did.

Each of those ships had four scout planes on board and they would be fired off the deck by catapults, elevated catapults. Later, in the war, those smaller planes would go out and scout for the enemy and relay information back to the ship. I didn't get a chance to go out and fly with those, but I paid a lot of attention to them and watched when they took off and made practice runs and circled around. The big ship I was on—all of them—would make a turn, make a slick in the water as a target, and the plane would come in and land on that slick and then taxi alongside the ship. They would lower a hoist from the ship, hoist up the plane, and bring it back on board. It was a great thing to watch and I took quite a few pictures of that.

By the time the trip ended it was the end of summer and time to go right back to school. I got some invitations to give lectures about the trip. I'm not sure how they came in, but I'm sure it was probably pushed along by my dad. Later, after I had been giving lectures for a while, I had an agent, Fred Hicks, who booked speakers. I was just one of many of them. I don't think that happened until my third year of giving lectures, though.

The very first illustrated lecture I had was a ski film. Not about the cruiser trip. Let's just say I was learning a great deal about the whole business of illustrated lecturing. My father was helping me. Illustrated lectures means showing a film and then talking as you go. They became popular as slide shows later. I stood on a platform or stage, greeted everybody, gave an introduction, and then the lights went down and the film came on. I stood off to the side and talked along with the film.

In the very beginning I was nervous, but I got so that I enjoyed it very much and I got good at it. The shows probably ran an hour and fifteen minutes or an hour and twenty minutes. The setup was usually a two-reel operation and when the first reel ran out you had an intermission. You set up the second reel in the projection booth while the audience took a break. Then after the second reel if anybody wanted to ask questions they could. I got pretty good at it, better and better over the years.

The best I can remember, the first time I gave an illustrated lecture I got twenty dollars. That was in the late thirties. It was something like that. I spoke to crowds of two hundred or three hundred—I can't recall what they paid to get in. I also gave the lectures in some high school auditoriums or school lecture halls. There would be a thousand people and they were all paying.

My first illustrated lecture was on skiing. It was not as sophisticated a production as the cruise trip and I gave that one on a pretty informal basis. I didn't get paid very much, but that's how I got started. My father kind of pushed me a little bit at first. Once I started doing it I liked it and improved, got more popular and in demand, and gave better lectures. I kept trying to put a little more humor into the films. My lecture on going around South America with the Navy was a better lecture than the ski lecture. In the late thirties, radio was a main form of entertainment and way to provide information. Television hadn't taken hold yet. Talking movies were only several years old. People who were looking for entertainment at night who wanted to go out of their homes were drawn to shows like illustrated lectures. It was quite a bit different than it is today with home computers, and so many television channels, and movie theaters with a dozen shows. A colored, illustrated lecture was a pretty popular thing in a big auditorium. You could blow up the picture quite large on a big screen, maybe fifteen feet wide, at least. You could do that at Carnegie Hall in New York, where I did lecture a couple of times.

Once I got the Navy lecture perfected I would go off from school over the weekend to deliver it, to put on a show somewhere. I went as far as Detroit. Sometimes I took the train and sometimes I flew. Commercial aviation was not that developed yet. I rode the rails an awful lot. I would get a night sleeper, an upper berth of some sort. I did that for a long time, even after I finished school and had other lectures, and after Tay and I were married she came with me.

When I was still in school I would catch a train on a Friday and ride into Detroit, or even Chicago, heading west. I'd get into a city and give a lecture on Saturday or Sunday, one per city, and then by Sunday night I would be back on the train heading east. I was studying and playing sports, so I already kept a hectic pace with my life. I didn't jump on trains to give lectures every weekend, but I did it several times. I didn't go away for weekends during the football season when we had games.

As young as I was and as long ago as that Navy tour was, I have always remembered it fondly. And I remember it well. It was also very important to my professional development. Some of the things I learned from Bonney Powell were things I used for the rest of my professional life in photography and moviemaking. And I did get an illustrated lecture out of the trip that I could use for years. Just having another film that was better than my ski film opened doors for me as a speaker. Once you get started and you put on a good show you gain a reputation. I had better material and was able to mold into it a good lecture.

That tour of South America with the Navy served me well for many years.

4

Climbing an
Alaskan Mountain at Sixteen

Mount Bertha is a 10,182-foot mountain in Alaska's Fairweather Range, located near the famous Glacier Bay in the southeast section of the state. A year after going to sea, Lowell Thomas Jr. was sixteen years old and he found himself on another adventure through his father's connections. This was a dramatically different trip from his months-long voyage with the US Navy.

One of Lowell Thomas Sr.'s good friends was a Bostonian named Bradford Washburn. They were kindred souls, both of them ready to take on any challenge, both of them not content to allow barriers to stay in their way if they wanted to accomplish things.

In a sense, Washburn, who had just become director of the Museum of Science, Boston, and would make it his life's work to expand and grow it, was more of a homebody than Thomas—with one exception. He was enamored of Alaska and almost every year in the thirties and after World War II, in pursuit of adventure and scientific achievement, he led expeditions to the north. Usually, the trips involved making an ascent of a previously unclimbed peak, and often mapping uncharted territory.

In 1940, Washburn, who had also been recently married to his secretary, Barbara, was planning an expedition to make the first ascent of Mount Bertha. Washburn was a meticulous planner and known for his safety record. If blizzards assaulted his teams he did not try to push on, but rather waited them out. His bride had never before climbed a mountain and he was determined to take her along, so Lowell Sr. couldn't help but feel comfortable entrusting his teen-aged son to Washburn's good judgment as well, despite the boy's total lack of mountaineering background. The one thing Lowell Jr. had going for him was a familiarity with snow and mountains from his skiing. This was something different from strapping on crampons and hoofing it up a big hill, but at the least it provided him with a sense of what it was like to visit higher elevations in cold weather.

This was a small-scale scientific-climbing expedition. The cast of characters on the journey consisted of Washburn, who was the leader; Barbara Washburn; Michel, an Austrian ski instructor; four Harvard University students; and the junior member of the crew, Lowell. Barbara Washburn had less exposure to the elements and outdoors than Thomas, though just as minimal an amount of climbing experience.

Bradford Washburn, who was the team leader and kept the official expedition diary, years later said, "I didn't expect this climb to be that challenging." He and Barbara had been married only two months and never had discussed climbing together. When he enlisted her for the Bertha climb, Washburn told her it would be "our Alaska honeymoon."

Looking back over the decades, Barbara Washburn, who only a short number of years later would become the first woman to climb Mount McKinley, at 20,320 feet the tallest mountain in North America, described how she believed Lowell Jr. came to join the group: "The son was in boarding school and Lowell [Sr.] felt that he could use an exciting adventure. Brad had a good reputation for bringing his expedition members home safely, but I always felt Lowell figured this trip wouldn't be too tough because Brad was bringing me along."

The expedition left Boston on June 20, 1940, and at that time it wasn't nearly as easy to fly to Alaska. The people, accompanied by sled dogs that would help transport people and gear later, departed by train for the north. For Lowell, the journey would be a sneak peek of Alaska long before he made what was then a territory and still almost two decades away from becoming a state, his future home.

◈ ◈ ◈

LOWELL: When the idea of my going and climbing a mountain was first mentioned, I didn't know a thing about Alaska. Nothing at all. I only knew that my father had been there many, many years ago when he was a young fellow before he was married. I didn't know anything about the place, but it sounded great to me with all of the mountains and glaciers and snow and being on skis. It was very appealing and it turned out to be a good summer. I met up with the Washburns in Boston, joined them there, and we all went along together to the north. That is when I met Barbara Washburn for the first time. We took the train to Seattle and then we boarded a boat in Seattle for Juneau.

On the journey I first heard a little bit about Mount Bertha, the objective of our trip. I was sixteen years old and thought I was in pretty good shape. I was in much better shape than I am now. I was sturdy at that point, probably about five feet ten inches tall and weighing about 175 pounds. I'd grown pretty quickly. I knew that there would be skiing and backpacking, carrying a lot of loads up glaciers. I was looking forward to it very much.

All of the other men on the trip had more experience in the outdoors than I did. They were all climbers and real outdoor guys. I was very much junior to them. I didn't really have any mountaineering experience. I had done a little bit of climbing, or hiking, in the Catskill Mountains in New York, but that was all. I went with the idea that I was going to climb to the summit like everyone else, but it didn't really matter that much to me. The trip was the thing. I was going on an expedition to Alaska—on glaciers, skiing. Whatever might happen was going to be great as far as I was concerned.

I didn't know how hard or easy it was going to be so I can't say what my anticipation was like. Once we arrived and got set up where we were going to ascend the mountain, it was good, hard slogging really, every day, carrying fifty-pound loads on your back up a glacier for a couple of hours onto the ice field and then back down, dodging crevasses as we went, trying to be careful. It was just wonderful. I loved it.

I enjoyed the company too. The Harvard students were great guys who got along famously. I felt like I was one of them even if I was very junior to them in age and experience. Mike the Austrian was a lot of fun to be with at all times. He was cracking jokes and talking about skiing. He told us about climbing in the Alps and trips he made in Europe. And Brad and Barbara Washburn were just fun to be with. I kidded with them a great deal.

They started calling me Casper as a nickname. That was because I was wearing a belt that had Casper, Wyoming, written on it. I'd gotten it from a cousin for Christmas, or something like that. So that was what they called me. "Hey, Casper, how are you doing today?" It was great to be in the wilderness. We were living in tents, cooking our own food over outdoor fires. We got our share of snowstorms. The snow blew in, but we didn't try to move in it. We got stuck for a few days in camp. We just sat there and waited for it to stop.

Brad was the leader and next in line I guess would be Maynard Miller, who had been a mountaineering guide out in Washington State on Mount Rainier. He was one of the Harvard seniors, but he had a lot of experience, so I would say he was sort of number two. Then there was Mike who had done some climbing in Austria. They were guys who really knew what they were doing. I just took instructions and just did whatever they asked me to do, carry loads, go along with so-and-so here up the glacier, just go along.

I learned a fair bit about mountaineering. I learned how to use an ice axe and how to dodge crevasses. It was all snow and ice climbing. We didn't have any rock climbing involved. We were roped up a portion of the time, especially going up the lower slopes. The terrain was all snow and ice and there was crevasse danger. I got up on the mountain probably at least halfway carrying the loads, but when it came to the upper hard part I stayed back down. That was because of the

At age sixteen, on a summer trip to climb Mount Bertha, Lowell Jr. made his first visit to Alaska, where he would later reside and become a bush pilot. Here he is in front of a Zodiac with expedition leader Bradford Washburn in Glacier Bay. *(Photo courtesy Barbara Washburn)*

difficulty of the climb. It would not have been the safest place for me to be without experience. The whole expedition was an adventure and it hadn't been my goal the way it had been for the others, to reach the summit of this mountain.

Mount Bertha was not as hard a mountain to climb as something like McKinley, but it had never been climbed before and there were plenty of winter challenges. There was plenty of bad weather to slow things up. The first time the lead group tried to reach the summit it turned back. Barbara told me she was scared at one point, but she always had a good attitude. At one point I asked Barbara if Brad was trying to kill her and she laughed. He was trying to get her to carry too much stuff and I knew she was just intent on working as hard as anyone else. She was the only woman on the trip and was sensitive to that and being there because she was the wife of the expedition leader. She was conscious of anybody thinking she didn't really belong, but that didn't happen.

Barbara was very much part of the team. She wasn't just standing off to the side waiting to do the cooking or anything like that. She carried her share of loads on the climbs and on the glaciers. I recall that. I probably took pity on her because she was struggling a little bit at one time when I said that about Brad. I must have thought it was kind of unfair to ask her to do that much. Barbara was not very big and she was carrying all of this weight. Brad would yell down at her like he would anyone else and she would yell back up at him and say something like, "Well, you know, I'm working here." She was just one of the gang. I remember her as very much part of the team, not an add-on. Barbara was conscious of keeping up with the boys, as she put it, and when the second summit attempt was made, she did get to the top along with Brad, Mike, and some of the Harvard guys.

It was quite a successful trip all around. Nobody got injured. Nobody fell down a crevasse. It went just great. We had flown to Glacier Bay by plane and then the airplane was used after that to drop supplies way, way up high at one point. We reached our jumping-off point by boat at the foot of a glacier on a terminal moraine. I just loved everything about it and I loved the idea of being in this wilderness, the wide-open expanse of mountains and glaciers and a new frontier. It got in my blood.

That was really my first taste of Alaska and something I remembered. It was a great trip, but it didn't turn me into a mountain climber. It did put me in love with glaciers and the wilderness. It became very natural for me to spend a lot of time on the Alaska glaciers and on the lower mountains of the Alaska Range. That was later, though. I had never aspired to be the type of mountaineer who went off to climb Mount Everest. By then I was starting to get the idea that I wanted to be a pilot like Jimmy Doolittle or Eddie Rickenbacker, though not in a war.

One thing that fascinated me when I was on Mount Bertha was how those small planes could operate and drop the food and supplies to us. They were floatplanes. I had been intrigued by aviation for some time and watched those scout planes on the Navy cruise quite closely. I was already deciding that I didn't want to be a naval pilot because if

Lowell discovered it was easy to work up an appetite in the wilderness on his Mount Bertha, Alaska, trip in 1940. *(Photo courtesy Barbara Washburn)*

you couldn't get back to your ship there was an awful lot of water out there. I wasn't tempted to join the navy for aviation, but I was starting to think that I wanted to go into the Army Air Corps. It seemed preferable to fly over land.

Jimmy Doolittle and Eddie Rickenbacker helped put the idea of flying into my head, but my interest was already established before they came to our house. My father was the historian of the first round-the-world flight conducted by four airmen in what was called the Army Air Service at the time. I was only a toddler in the late twenties. Later, my father and I coauthored a book called *Famous First Flights That Changed History: Sixteen Dramatic Adventures*, and that adventure was reported in there.

I may have been little, but I heard a lot about the flight. After the flight was over, some of the flyers came to the farm to talk to my dad and they were telling the story a lit bit fuller. He wasn't on the actual flight, but met them at several points along the way, as I recall. Anyway, it seemed to me to be pretty fascinating, the things these guys were talking about, their experiences of flying around the world. I wanted very much to become a part of it.

It got in my blood very early on, all of it, the flying, the airplanes, being up in the air, cruising along. Frank Hawkes was another one who was a famous pilot who visited us. He was a member of my father's softball team. I saw quite a lot of him. He would fly in sometimes and land on the nearby golf course. All of that had a great influence on me when I was growing up.

The funny part is, though, that I can't remember the first time I was on an airplane for sure. I would have been quite young, traveling with my parents. It was probably a trip on a DC-3 as a passenger.

So every few years or so, for one reason or another, whether it was visits from famous pilots to our home, to my father chronicling these adventures, to me seeing the Navy planes, to me watching the planes work in Alaska, something was happening that led me closer and closer to a career in aviation.

The trip to Mount Bertha was something memorable. It was a great experience and adventure at the time, but there was no way then that it seemed as if I would ever come to live in Alaska and make it my home for half of my life. That was the furthest thing from my mind at the time and almost twenty years passed before I returned to the state and moved to Alaska.

5

College and the Military

By the time Lowell Thomas Jr. finished high school at The Taft School he looked at the world as a wide, wide place indeed. Besides being exposed to some of the most fascinating people in the universe right in his own home because they were guests of his father, Lowell had a couple of great adventure trips under his belt from the Navy cruise and the Alaska mountaineering expedition. He did not know what he wanted to be when he grew up, but his interests pointed to photography and cinematography in the same kind of storytelling vein that Lowell Thomas Sr. employed. But Lowell Jr. was passionate about aviation as well, and hoped that an opportunity would arise to get started in that same field some way.

At this age, in his late teens, Lowell was also enamored of skiing and he wanted to attend college in a place where he might have the chance to become a competitive skier. This was an era when college athletic recruiting was virtually nonexistent for sports teams, with the possible exception, depending on the school, of football teams and some basketball teams. An athlete might procure a university-supplied part-time job to work his way through the required payments of tuition and room and board, but the phrase "full ride" was not yet in use.

Unlike some high school grads who wish to get as far away from home as soon as possible, Lowell did not have that on his list of criteria. He wanted to attend a good school where he could obtain a good education and ski too. The perfect location for his needs seemed to be Dartmouth College, the Ivy League school in New Hampshire, and that's where he enrolled in the fall of 1940 as a freshman.

By that time Adolf Hitler had invaded Poland and war was raging in Europe. Only the most naïve isolationists believed that the United States would not be drawn into the war. Tensions increased in the Pacific, as well, and when the Japanese bombed Pearl Harbor on December 7, 1941, Americans were officially combatants in World War II.

Although he could not have foreseen how these world events were going to play out when he signed up for college, soon enough Lowell Thomas Jr. would be receiving lessons in how to fly planes and was on his way to becoming a pilot.

❖ ❖ ❖

LOWELL: I think that my father hoped that it might work out that I ended up working for the State Department.

My father and I were close. He was a great influence on my life and he had a great impact on me when I was growing up. When he began doing his nightly broadcasts from the farm, from our home, I was around a lot watching and listening. He put me to use from time to time. I spent a lot of time sitting next to him when he was on the air, putting down cards each minute so he could keep track of where he was in the broadcast, how much time he had. I was exposed to broadcasting that way. I was always impressed by him. He was a very, very fine father. He was always looking out for my best interest. He was full of ideas for me, sometimes too many, I used to think.

He often seemed to be working at arranging my future life a bit. I was exposed to more things at a younger age than I would have been and met a lot of interesting people. It wasn't always fun, though. Sometimes it was a pain in the neck when those interesting people came over and the family was sort of pushed aside. I was a little bit jealous many times, in many cases when he was involved with other people instead of being involved with me directly. But he was a good father who spent an awful lot of time with me and as I got older he spent even more time with me.

One thought was that I might go to Yale. It was pretty close to Pawling, New York, only an hour-and-a-half drive. That was a possibility, but I didn't really want to go to Yale because it was in New Haven, another city. I liked the country. I never applied anywhere else except to Dartmouth. My grades were good enough. It was not only my first choice, but my only choice. Hanover is a small New Hampshire town with really nice people. Good country, mountains and almost endless trails, and academically we were on a par with any other college. I became a freshman at Dartmouth and was busy with classes and skiing. I also joined a fraternity. It was Delta Kappa Epsilon, DKE. It was called the Deke House.

Pearl Harbor brought the United States into the war and from then on it was only a matter of when we were going to be in the military. I became an aviation cadet in 1943 and after my lengthy instruction flew my first plane, a Boeing Stearman, as a member of the Air Force, which was then part of the Army. The Air Force didn't become independent as a branch of service until after World War II.

During the first stage of instruction we didn't fly. We were on the ground. It took quite a while before we were checked out and then they turned us loose to solo and practice in the Stearman, which was a biplane with one engine and two open cockpit seats.

There were four stages as a cadet. One was preflight where you went through the military flight instruction, learned about Morse code and engines, all of the technical things. Then you went to primary flight school and that's where we flew the Stearman. We had about sixty hours of flight time in that single-engine plane. Then you were sent to basics. In basics you flew bigger planes. Again they were single-engine, but much more powerful engines. We were there for four to six weeks. The next step was advanced instruction in twin-engine planes. I was in Columbus, Mississippi, for that. After that I learned how to fly

B-25s, the bombers. Once you completed that part of the course you were prepared to be a combat pilot.

Not everyone who wanted to fly could learn to fly. A lot of people washed out along the way. The challenge is there, but not everyone is cut out to be a pilot. I was and I was pretty adept at it. When I was younger I had learned about speed and working with cars. Other guys who came straight in had no background or training or experience. You followed the instruction and the instructor. Your instructor would demonstrate maneuvers and then ask you to do it. You would try it a couple of times until you finally learned how to do it. Then you just kept practicing those maneuvers. You had to kind of suck in your gut a little bit when you were going upside down and doing spins and snap rolls.

These were not tricks you did for fun. You were supposed to make those moves. You had to. The purpose was to demonstrate that you could completely control the airplane. If something happened you had to pull out of it, to know what to do in order to get out of a spin. It was a pretty exciting business. We had parachute training too, on what to do in a crisis, in case something went wrong and you had to bail out. I never had to do it. I never had to jump.

Once I got started in the training, especially after my longstanding interest in aviation, I very much enjoyed it. I just loved it. I think I was a pretty fast learner because I enjoyed it so much. I was coordinated. I think some guys were not very good at parts of the training because they were not coordinated. It was pretty tough. Some guys got sick, threw up, and just really couldn't hack it. I loved it.

Everyone in the service wanted to go into combat and fight to defend the country, whether it was in Europe or in the Pacific. I wanted to go and do my part against the Japanese or the Germans. I felt more hostility towards the Japanese because of Pearl Harbor, but it just didn't work out that way.

All of that time I was preparing I thought I was going to war. I thought I was going into pursuit flying, where we would chase enemy aircraft. I was hoping to do it. However, when I finished all of the cadet stages I was asked to stay behind to become an instructor. I was pretty

An aviation cadet in the Army Air Corps during World War II, Lowell Jr. learned to fly and became a flight instructor.

upset about that at the time, but looking back I guess it was a compliment because they thought I had done well enough to be a teacher. I never left the United States. There was a new commander who decided. I just wanted to be part of the action. I guess I was like a kid in many respects.

I wasn't very old at that point. I was twenty or twenty-one. I had finished a year or so of college. But the powers-that-be had two reasons to make me an instructor. One of them was I guess they felt that I would be good at it. They were confident about that. The other reason was that I spoke some French. At about the same time there were some Free Frenchmen, some of General Charles de Gaulle's people, who had come over to train to become pilots. Maybe somebody looked at my paperwork and saw my background and said, "Oh, he speaks French" and that's why they wanted me around too. The reality was that although I had taken some French in school I didn't know enough French to be really helpful for those guys. But the bosses probably felt that having somebody around who spoke some French was better than having somebody around who had no French at all.

During this period of being an instructor I had the first flying close call of my life among the million-plus miles I flew in airplanes. I was flying a B-25 with three students aboard. We were doing touch-and-go landings and long landings with the slow application of power. We lifted off as the last flare pot on the runway slipped by. We were following normal procedure of leveling off until critical single-engine speed of about 120 miles per hour. Suddenly, I wondered what was ahead in the total darkness and flipped on the landing lights (which we were not supposed to use during this simulated front-line training). We were supposed to land only with the runway lights and no landing lights. That was part of the training because during war those might be the circumstances that you face.

The idea was that if you had your lights on the enemy might see you. We were landing in the darkness with just smudge pots along the side of the runway. This one particular student that I had in the left seat while I was in the right seat as instructor, landed a little bit long and he was a little bit slow getting going again. He was putting on the power again and the light went on in my mind: the landing light, a powerful wing light that shines straight out.

There rose a stand of pine trees at the edge of the forest, only a few seconds away. I had just enough time to pull back on the control wheel and we zoomed up and over the trees. Flying straight into that forest would almost certainly have been fatal. If I had waited, oh, who knows, another fifteen or twenty seconds, we might not have had time to get over them. God surely intervened. I got a little religion out of that, I really did. That was the first really close call of my piloting career. We had used that field a number of times, but in the daytime. That was the difference.

While I was in the military there were some other close calls giving flight instruction. Some of those came while flying at night and while trying to teach cadets how to fly in formation without running into the plane as you were forming up. That meant there were always tricky moments. There are three aircraft together, the lead plane, the one on the left, and the one on the right. There were some nervous moments.

By not actually going to war, by not participating in combat and dropping bombs, I ended up gaining all of the benefits of aviation training that helped me for the rest of my life, without the downsides. I didn't have to see the grimy, dirty side of aviation, bombing people or shooting other pilots. What I had learned in aviation through the Air Corps stayed with me into my eighties.

I did not return to Dartmouth until 1946. By then I had been in the service and was older, going on twenty-three and no longer in that ordinary eighteen-to-twenty-two-year-old typical college demographic. Although I was in a fraternity and on the ski team I was like most of the other students who came back after World War II. It got to be one of those things where you want to finish up your degree and get on about your life.

You're older now. The fraternity business is kind of old hat. You had sort of been in a fraternity in the military. It was a different experience coming out of the war and going back to college than it had been coming out of high school and going into college. We wanted to get the best education we could and move on, find a job, and get married.

I still liked Dartmouth. I lived in the fraternity house and the skiing was great. Later, my daughter went to Dartmouth and was on the ski team and my son went to Dartmouth and he was on the ski team.

Not that I was sure what kind of job I would go after. The idea of joining the State Department was still alive. I was attracted by foreign affairs. I signed up to go to graduate school at the Woodrow Wilson School of Public and International Affairs at Princeton.

Right after I graduated from Dartmouth I had an unusual experience with the Air Force in 1948. I was recalled to participate in a trip by Secretary of the Air Force Stuart Symington. It had a kinship with the type of mission I was involved with when I was fifteen. The trip I took the first time was with the Navy to South America. This was a trip by airplane to other parts of the world. We flew in four-engine planes, large military planes, C-40s, again with dignitaries. There were two planes that traveled together. This was another one of those goodwill missions like the one I was on when I was younger, only this time by plane instead of ship. One of the planes carried a lot of luggage and equipment while the other one carried most of the dignitaries. I was lucky enough to be with those people most of the time. It was a pretty frantic trip because we didn't stay terribly long anywhere. We kept moving all of the time.

We gathered in California and started by flying to Hawaii. We stopped at Midway Island (where there had been a major World War II battle), China, Burma, India, the Mediterranean, Europe, and back to the United States. There was always a great deal of pageantry on these goodwill missions and cocktail parties. Luckily I had already learned to drink on that other mission. I handled beer alright, and cigars, though I didn't like them much. There were parties where all the local dignitaries showed up to meet with Secretary of the Air Force Symington.

One thing that was on the agenda was a nuclear test at Bikini Atoll. I was there for that, but at the same time not anywhere near the actual explosion. Symington and the other high poo-bahs were in a plane wearing very dark glasses, watching what happened. That was one of the keys of the trip. The United States had already dropped the atomic bomb on Hiroshima and Nagaski and ended World War II. This trip was again about showing the flag and, with the backdrop of the bomb maybe making the point that those countries should stick with us rather than aligning with the Communist Soviet Union.

It was quite something to be called to go on that trip. One of the things I did was communicate with my father at home and feed him information for his newscasts. That type of thing was probably why they invited me in the first place, although I did have the experience from the previous trip on the cruiser and did take pictures. My father had the number one radio newscast in the country. [He asked me] to send reports back to him via shortwave radio. In fact, one of the side projects of the trip was checking out the shortwave radio capabilities of the places we visited. I sent back reports that were a couple of minutes long, three or four times, which he used in his evening broadcasts. They could have invited anyone else. There were other good cameramen out there, far better than myself.

We moved at a whirlwind pace. We didn't stay very long anywhere, maybe a day or two at the most, and then we were off to the next place and more dignitaries would come on board and we'd go ashore and have parties. That's just the way it was in each place.

There was just enough time off the plane to see some of the local sites. I liked the Philippines. We saw Angkor Wat, the largest Hindu temple in the world, in Cambodia. I saw quite a few ancient temples and they were very impressive. China was still unsettled. Mao Zedong was still leading the revolt in the countryside. It was not until the next year that he established the People's Republic of China. In 1948, Chiank Kai-Shek was still in charge. He didn't flee to Taiwan till the next year.

World War II was still fresh in the minds of people, but we didn't encounter any ruins that I remember as things were being rebuilt. There was lots of poverty, especially in India and China, beggars on the street. I was struck by the size of the crowds in the street in China. Besides the beggars in the street in India there were also cows in the street. As we know, the cows in India are sacred. They mingled with the people. That was a little striking in the beginning. In China it was striking to see the guys pulling rickshaws that were tremendously laden down with loads, pulling by themselves instead of having a pony or a mule to do the pulling. That was pretty hard work pulling those big loads and you knew they weren't living on steak—probably all rice.

The trip probably took a month and although it moved along so swiftly I got a lot out of it. First there was the travel, which was great, and then there was my interest in foreign affairs. There I was on a diplomatic mission with the Secretary of the Air Force. I had an interest in the Foreign Service and the idea of the travel appealed to me. I'm sure my father's influence played a part too. I was thinking that would be the best way to go if I was to enter one of the regular careers. But then I decided, even with more schooling, that I was doing very well speaking and making films for illustrated lectures and that I'd probably stay with that.

6

Going to Work

After Lowell Thomas Jr. graduated from Dartmouth College in 1948, he chose to further his education in a nontraditional setting doing more work in a hands-on fashion, although he did also begin graduate work at Princeton. He continued giving illustrated lectures.

Lowell did not take after his father in terms of becoming a broadcaster and working on the radio, but he did share some of his interests. Lowell Jr. did want to tell stories, did want to make films, did wish to keep on giving narrations and he definitely wanted to travel as much as possible in the United States and throughout the world. He had a great appetite for covering the miles and relaying the most curious and entertaining tales about what he saw after he returned from his travels. Lowell not only shot still photographs by the thousand, he recorded thousands of feet of film.

One aspect of filmmaking that promised to make it more exciting and dramatic was the development of Cinerama. Credit for inventing Cinerama—combining the words cinema and panorama—was given to Fred Waller, but further development was attributed to Merian C. Cooper, who worked closely with Lowell Thomas Sr. The process was used for widescreen filming based on three synchronized 35-millimeter projectors. Cinerama was very big around the Thomas household. Lowell Sr. was actively involved in making some of the first Cinerama films and Lowell Jr. began working with Cooper and Lowell Sr. on their projects. At a time when he was still a young man and uncertain of precisely what career path to follow, in the late forties and early fifties, Lowell hooked himself to the Cinerama train.

❖ ❖ ❖

LOWELL: I have always enjoyed travel inside the country and outside the country and this job enabled me to travel. I enjoyed that life very much. I was the advance man for these projects. One of them took me to Salt Lake City where we wanted to film the Mormon Tabernacle Choir.

When I could, I did my own illustrated lecture tours. I went everywhere, to just about every state. I spoke in big cities in Texas, in Los Angeles, San Francisco, Chicago, Detroit, in Canada, as well.

Mostly I traveled by train and sometimes by plane. Commercial aviation was still getting established and a lot of the committees that hired me for talks were still nervous about people coming by plane.

After a while I had a Pontiac van and a driver and my own arc projector, though in the beginning I relied on local equipment and local projectionists. Once in a while things went wrong. A bulb might burn out on a projector and there might not be a spare. Other times I might have a little extra intermission because the film broke and it had to be rethreaded.

I don't remember having to call things off completely. We had extra intermissions, but we never had total failure. There were repairs in the middle of the show that could take a while and I'd say it was fairly standard. It might happen about every third lecture. That's pretty often. I'd have to be ready to chat with the audience for a while, get them to ask questions and whatnot. In government they call that a filibuster.

The illustrated lecture was a pretty big thing in those days. Sometimes I got to a place and the crowd would be fifteen hundred people in a pretty big auditorium. I had to get used to that and treat the crowds all the same, big or small. I don't remember any bad times when almost nobody showed up. The bad times were when there was a technical breakdown.

After a while I was so familiar with some of the lectures that I could give them without any lights or without having to read anything. I enjoyed it. I suppose I got a little bit bored with doing the same lecture after a while, but I always got pretty good feedback. It was my job as a speaker to make them happy, so if they were happy, I was happy to make them happy.

You could tell how interested an audience was and when they were interested that was gratifying. I enjoyed entertaining them. I think I hit every state eventually. I went to a lot of university towns. Maybe not for lectures, but for filming and information gathering. I have been to a lot of different countries too: China, Russia, Nepal, Tibet, which was a country at one time, all through Europe and South America, New Zealand, Australia. I'm not sure which ones I've missed. There are a lot of new countries since the sixties. If you watch the opening ceremonies in the Olympics you will see flags from countries you never heard of before. I think I saw that there were more than 150 countries in the Summer Olympics in 2012.

I was working as an advance man on Cinerama stuff and giving my illustrated lectures when I first met Tay in 1948. Her maiden name is Pryor and our families knew one another. Her father was the vice president of Pan American Airlines and my father knew him well. I had just come home from a string of lectures and we were all invited to eat dinner at the Pryors' in Connecticut. That was how we met and hit it off.

Tay was attending Smith College in Northampton, Massachusetts, and I went to visit her there. We spent some time together there and our relationship just kept growing. We knew each other for about a year and a half before we got married in the spring of 1950. Our anniversary is May 20.

Tay also had a strong desire to travel. She had done a major college paper on Africa, a mountain range there. Not Kilimanjaro but the Rwenzori Mountains on the border between Uganda and the Congo.

We both wanted to travel and we both were aviation-minded too. So it worked out well.

In 1949, on one of my filming adventures, I was in Iran. I was making a film there and I received a telegram from my father. It basically said to stop what I was doing and to meet him in Calcutta immediately.

My father had made a practice over the years of going where no one else went. That's how he met up with Lawrence of Arabia. As a correspondent in World War I he asked to be sent to a theater of war that as few other people as possible were covering. When he got to the desert he learned there were only two other correspondents around and neither of them were paying the slightest bit of attention to what Lawrence was accomplishing.

During the first half of the twentieth century (still true today, but not so much), there were closed countries that didn't allow any foreigners or tourists. My father was well known for his broadcast work in the United States, and he always hoped to benefit from having a famous name when he wanted to visit somewhere that Westerners were not welcome, but there were never any guarantees. With some countries my dad tried over and over again for years to gain admittance, but was constantly rebuffed. Some time would pass and he would seek an invitation once again, or he would make clear it was a standing request. World politics changed over time and sometimes they changed to his benefit. Whereas some place was closed for a long time and did not welcome strangers for years, things changed and suddenly he was welcome.

For many years my father had been fascinated with Tibet. He had long wanted to visit. He tried to obtain an official invitation or permission, but could never get it approved. It was sort of a standing desire with him. He definitely wanted to go to Tibet, but Tibet definitely didn't want him to come. It was nothing personal, but it was the state policy of Tibet to remain withdrawn behind its own gates, to retain its privacy. Over the centuries several explorers wanted to visit Tibet for different reasons. Some of them—a very few—sneaked into the country, though given how homogeneous Tibet was with little variation in the people, it was impossible to escape notice for very long if you were a taller, white, blue-eyed foreigner, or something akin to that. It was Tibet's choice not to interact with the world at large. Much of the motivation behind this was religious. Tibet was a religious state, immersed in Buddhism. Government officials feared that if Westerners or other visitors came to Tibet regularly their ways would rub off and essentially pollute the purity of the system in Tibet. The country had not modernized, but that too was pretty much by design. In a place where religion was paramount in the people's daily lives it was agreed that modern amenities were unnecessary and would just be distractions. The goal was always to preserve Buddhism from being diluted, first and foremost.

Although he never stopped trying, it got to the point where it seemed as if my father would never get into Tibet and be welcomed officially. Then, in 1949, while I was in Iran and my father was in New York, he was notified that he was being invited to visit Tibet. The Dalai Lama had put his stamp of approval on my father's application. Originally, my father wanted to bring me and a camera crew with him, make a full-fledged expedition into Tibet with scientists, geologists, and so on. When approval was issued for the trip—effective more or less immediately—he was also informed "nothing doing" on his plans to put together a major expedition. My dad was told that he would be allowed to come to Tibet, but he could bring only one other person with him, "your son if you want to." So that was it. It was going to be the two of us or nothing. Of course my father accepted under those conditions and asked me to join him. He pretty much assumed that I would want to go, which I did.

This time when my father sent forth his proposal for permission to enter Tibet he approached the Tibetans through the Indian government. My father's contact in the Indian government was someone he had known quite well in New York when he had been stationed at the United Nations. This diplomat, who had lived in the United States, passed the word along and recommended that if the Tibetans were going to let anybody come from America they should let my father in because he was in an outstanding position to tell the world about the country.

I was making a film in Iran about the early days in Persia, and Turkey, and the whole region, a project that I had been working on over time. I was compiling material for a new illustrated lecture and while I was there Justice William O. Douglas just showed up. He and his son were going to take a trek with back-area tribesman, just for adventure. He was an extraordinary man who had the longest term ever on the Supreme Court of more than thirty-six years, and he was a very active environmentalist. He wrote books, but I don't know if he wrote about this trek he took.

I heard he was there and he heard I was there, so he invited me to come along with him for a few days while he was traveling with the tribesmen. They were very primitive people, desert people with goats and sheep. They were just living off the land, very poor. They milked their goats and in the winter they moved to where it was warmer and drier by the Indus River, close to India and Pakistan. In the summer they moved back to the hills where the grass was nice and green and wet and the goats and sheep could feed on the grass. They were completely nomadic. They had horses and some donkeys, not camels. A lot of them were just plain on foot. I filmed all of that and used it in my illustrated lecture. That was one of the highlights of the film. The audiences were so interested in how the people lived in nomadic fashion and how they had so little.

William O. Douglas was a swell fellow really. He was a very nice guy to get along with. I liked him very much indeed. He did not seem like a justice of the Supreme Court, not while he was with me in the desert. Just a very pleasant man. Back in the United States when I saw his name in the newspapers connected to the news or court decisions I would always think back and be reminded of him in the bush. It was kind of neat.

My father sent a note to the US Embassy and somehow they found me to deliver it. My father's telegram read, "Meet me in Calcutta as soon as you can." It sounded like the name of a spy book actually.

I loved the sound of that and I was excited because Tibet was a big thing in my mind too.

The instructions were to drop everything and head to India, which on its northern border abuts Tibet. Calcutta would be our jumping-off place where gear was to be assembled and where our approach to Lhasa, the Tibetan capital, was to be organized. At 11,450 feet, Lhasa is one of the highest cities in the world in altitude. We would have to practice our deep breathing.

My father would join me in Calcutta. It took him a little bit longer since he was traveling from New York. The approval [to enter Tibet] was a pleasant shock. This was something on his to-do list for a long time, something that was fading from the realm of likelihood of ever happening. The idea had been stored away over time, but now my father could reach for it on the shelf and bring it back to life. It was not really my dream that we were living, but I was very excited all the same knowing it was something very important to my father and Tibet was also someplace otherwise beyond my reach to visit.

Coming and going and visiting took months. But the trip to Tibet was rewarding, exciting, and one of the great adventures of my life. It still captivates me in thought more than a half century later. It is also a trip where a major accident added more drama than we needed to the itinerary and that we were fortunate did not end with the death of my father in the middle of barren lands on a halfway carved-out trail between Tibet and India

7

To the Forbidden Roof
of the World

Throughout its history Tibet sought to be left alone. It was a religious country, focused on Buddhism and did not consider itself to be part of China. The nation was a cold and snowy land, tucked into a corner of the world where it was not really on the way to anywhere. That helped preserve the privacy its rulers craved.

By the late 1940s the world had passed Tibet by and that was the way Tibet wanted it. There was no modern airport to approach by flight. Automobile travel to Tibet and in Tibet was not possible because there were no modern roads. The altitude in Tibet was extreme, even higher in the hinterlands, reaching fourteen to eighteen thousand feet. Tibet was pretty much surrounded by desert or mountains. It was a difficult nation to reach and it didn't want anyone to come anyway.

Only a tiny number of foreigners had penetrated Tibet's defenses in recent centuries and mostly as soon as they were found out they were tossed out of the country. According to research done by Lowell Jr. before the expedition began, when two Army officers met with the Dalai Lama in 1942, they were only the fourth and fifth Americans to ever have such an audience.

Ordinarily, Lowell and his father would not expect to see any other foreigners in Tibet when they arrived. But a recent exception to the longstanding rule of isolation had been made and as it so happened the Thomases would overlap with the two most famous foreign visitors to the country.

Residing in Lhasa when the Thomases set out on their trip to Tibet were Heinrich Harrer and Peter Aufschnaiter, Austrian mountain climbers who had departed their home in 1939 as part of a four-man group determined to make the first ascent of the Himalayan peak Nanga Parbat. Nanga Parbat is one of the world's limited number of 26,000-foot mountains. If the team had conquered its summit that would have been the first mountain of such height climbed, but it was turned back by storms.

The group retreated and just as it planned to embark for home, World War II broke out and the climbers were incarcerated by the British. After five years and several attempts to escape, the climbers were successful, but when they broke out of the prison camp they split into small groups. In the end, after hardships and long miles of trekking Aufschnaiter and Harrer made their way to Tibet. It took until January of 1946 for them to reach Lhasa and there they stayed. Harrer became the personal tutor of the Dalai Lama and eventually upon returning to Europe he wrote the best-selling book *Seven Years in Tibet*, which decades later, starring Brad Pitt as Harrer, became a popular movie.

The Dalai Lama, the religious and political leader of Tibet, had just turned fourteen in 1949 when he agreed to allow the Thomases to enter his country, broadcast from Tibet, and then bring the country's story to the world after exiting.

❖ ❖ ❖

LOWELL: When I received the urgent missive from my father I dropped what I was doing in Iran. I would never have said that I was too busy doing something else. As quickly as I could, I made my way to India, met my father, and we worked out some basic arrangements through our embassy and through the Indian government.

My second jumping-off point for Tibet was to be Gangtok, the capital of Sikkim Province. Gangtok was a center of Buddhist learning and culture and had been for some time. A monastery was built there in 1840 and that began the strong connection with the religion. Gangtok was fairly close to the Tibetan border and that is where we gathered the equipment we needed and put together a travel party of a few pack animals and some porters to create a small caravan. First we had to purchase our supplies, which fell to me, and do that in Calcutta, and then get them to Gangtok.

I gathered the equipment that had to sustain us. If I forgot anything essential it would be just our bad luck. No motels or lunch wagons along this trail. Our equipment included saddles and bridles, army cots and sleeping bags, mosquito netting, flashlights, a portable table, two portable chairs, a canvas bath, tarpaulins to keep packs dry, and ski pants, ski boots, woolen shirts, sweaters, windbreakers, and rubberized rain suits. A first-rate medical kit is a must on an extended journey into remote country where there is no modern medicine.

In Calcutta I rounded up a complete kitchen, everything from pots and pans to dish towels. The most important kitchen item was the portable primus cooker made in America, which I had with me in Iran. We expected to live off the land to some extent, but to be on the safe side I bought enough food to keep us going for more than a month. At the Great Eastern grocery store I made up eight cases of food, each case weighing sixty-five pounds, each containing enough food to last both of us for six days.

While we seemed to be well equipped, it was not as if we were dining on the type of cuisine we might find in a fancy restaurant in New York City. Breakfast on the road to Lhasa would consist of stewed prunes or apple rings, followed by a large bowl of oatmeal or Cream of Wheat, canned bacon, crackers, jam, and butter. As for liquids, we could have our choice of Ovaltine, coffee, tea or cocoa, topped off with powdered milk and sugar. Lunch, which we expected to eat in the saddle, would be simple but concentrated: crackers and cheese, sardines, chocolate, dried raisins, dates, and figs. Our big meal was to come in the evening at the end of a long, fatiguing day of hiking and riding. After a bowl of bouillon we would have more buttered crackers and jam, then a plate of hot canned roast beef, veal, or salmon, together with any fresh vegetables that we could buy along our way. Dessert would usually be dried fruit again, since Tibet is too cold to grow fruit, except for some peaches and apricots in the warmer, low-lying eastern valleys. Then we drank more tea, cocoa, or Ovaltine.

When an expedition bound for Tibet leaves Calcutta it looks like Ringling Bros. and Barnum & Bailey emerging from winter quarters. But against an Asian background it is even more colorful than the circus. We left the last night of July for the railroad center of Siliguri at the foot of the mighty Himalayas, three hundred miles north of Calcutta. The last sixteen miles of the journey to Gangtok was by jeep.

It was not until we actually reached Gangtok that we received our final clearance to enter Tibet. Waiting for us was a message reading, "With reference to Mr. Lowell Thomas, United States national, and his son—although the Tibetan government does not usually allow foreign visitors to come to Lhasa—in view of friendly relations between the Tibetan government and the government of the USA, they have been granted permission for these two to enter the country." It was signed for the Dalai Lama by Tsepon Shakabpa, the man who headed the first Tibetan trade mission to the United States in the summer of 1948.

The group consisted of me and my father; an interpreter named Tsewong Namgyal; and a cook, Tsewang Norbu; plus the sirdar (or leader of the porters), Lajor; and a small number of porters who changed as we went, but usually two or three at a time. The trip merely to reach Tibet was an adventure of its own. The terrain was very rugged, rocky, and barren, no snow where we rode on horseback, but no real trails to speak of either.

An interpreter was going to be all-important. The Tibetan people, who are short and sturdy in stature, had not had their origins completely pinpointed. They were believed to be part Mongolian, and part Burmese and Assamese. The language had similarities to Burmese, but it was nothing like the English alphabet at all.

When we reached the India-Tibet border we were surprised not to find it manned by military officials. Before we saw anyone at

14,800-foot Nathu La we saw three bushy-tailed wild yaks. Even if no officials gazed upon us suspiciously, these animals did. We were inside Tibet, at last. Actually, the border seemed to run through the town, so it wasn't until we were on the downhill side of the settlement that we were truly in Tibet. We dismounted and walked. There is an old Tibetan saying that goes, "If he doesn't carry you uphill, he is no horse, and if you don't walk down, you are no man."

The only two Westerners were me and my dad. That was wonderful because we were close together and really had some more father and son time than we had for a few years. We had the first battery-driven tape recorder with us and my father did a number of reports from along the trail on one-quarter-inch tape. He was able to send the tapes back to India by porter who traveled overland to deliver them. The guy carried the tape in his backpack and ran to the nearest village to deliver the tape. That's the way they still did it then. It was very rustic, very rudimentary living. The tape went to India and then was sent to New York. Eventually it would appear on my father's program—he had other people doing the program—while he was away. They would introduce it like this: "Well, Lowell Thomas is off in Tibet and here's his latest report." Then they would run three or four minutes of tape about where we had been.

It is difficult to convey the excitement that I felt on this trip. We had a caravan of our own, just me and my father, traveling through wild country with foreign porters accompanying us into forbidden territory. It had the feel of adventure and romance to it.

From what we heard later the radio audience ate it up. They thought it was something to hear about such an exotic place that had been sealed up for so many years. People knew about Shangri-La from the book James Hilton wrote, *Lost Horizon,* and to them it sounded as if we were going to a real Shangri-La—and we were. The Shangri-La in the book was fictional, but it described a happy valley in the Himalayas that people considered to be a paradise. It sounded quite a bit like what we were doing.

Until we set out from India to Lhasa even we could not comprehend how remote the Tibetan capital was. On the maps of the time the

In of their great feats from their 1949 journey to Tibet, Lowell Thomas Sr.,
with the assistance of Lowell Jr., managed to make some live radio broadcasts
back to the United States. They sometimes had to work by candlelight.

word *Tibet* was printed over a gigantic swath of territory, so we knew it
was large. But it was about as inaccessible as Antarctica. Everyone considered Antarctica the toughest place to reach on the planet, but it took
longer to get from one of Tibet's neighbors to the capital than to journey
by sea from South America to the Antarctic.

The journey consisted of about 50 percent of the time walking
and 50 percent of the time on horseback. You couldn't stay in the saddle all the time. You wouldn't want to. We got off and walked a lot. It
was very slow going. We were only going a couple of miles an hour and
we were climbing all of the time. We were going higher and higher.
The highest pass was something like 16,200 feet. We acclimated as we
went because of our pace so the altitude didn't bother us at all. We were
making ten or twelve miles a day of progress, not very much. It was
definitely slow going. One thing we were warned about was to try to
make it across the bleak, open country to a small settlement by the end

of each day, if only because we were going to have to keep renting additional pack animals so they did not work themselves to exhaustion.

Sometimes we arrived in a village late at night and everyone was asleep. Other times we were greeted by individuals that smiled at us. Everyone was polite and there was curiosity to see us because foreigners never came their way. They knew we were guests of the Dalai Lama. The only conversation was through our interpreter, but there was very little of that. Overall we had little interaction with these people while we were on the trail.

Once we got through the Himalayas and onto the great plains of Tibet it went a little bit faster. We had dropped down to an altitude of about twelve thousand feet after being up higher and on these Tibetan plateaus we were very well acclimated. We just moved along there, probably made twenty or twenty-two miles in a day.

The scenery was spectacular. We were in the Himalayas, so we were surrounded by the tallest mountains in the world. They were all snow covered. Kangchenjunga, the third highest mountain in the world at 28,169 feet, dominated the range. There were also roaring rivers and streams going by. We were on very narrow trails where the animals had to be very careful where they stepped. The trail might only be four or five feet wide. On one side there would be a rock wall and on the other side a drop of thousands of feet down. We didn't lose any animals, but we were told that they had lost pack animals on those trails. They just stepped wrong and went over the side to their deaths.

One of the greatest aggravations of the journey—shades of Alaska—was being pounced upon by bugs. Leeches, tiny bloodsuckers, as thin as horsehairs, that were about an inch long, set out to feast upon us. With our thicker rain gear my father and I fared very well if we saw them drop on us. We could flick them off. Our porters did not do as well.

We encountered a tremendous amount of rain. Some of the pathways were better than others. Some were made up of a kind of flagstones that were pretty level and the horses could step easily over them. Other times we were on muddy hills with large rocks protruding and could only make slow progress.

It was rugged going on the trail to Lhasa to see the Dalai Lama in Tibet in 1949, and heading back to India, and at one point Lowell Thomas Sr., shown here, was thrown from his horse and seriously injured. He credits Lowell Jr. for saving his life in the wilderness.

We crossed into the Chumbi Valley and came to our first Buddhist monastery, Kagyu Gompa. This was one of the homes of the Red Hat monks. That was one of the sects of Buddhism in Tibet. It was there that we secured our Tibetan passports, called lamyik, and were introduced to the local trade agent. Three servants arrived bearing gifts, including a tray piled with eggs, a butchered and dressed shoulder of yak, and a big bowl of yak butter. When we received the gift of those platters of eggs, some of them were to eat and some of them were ceremonial and quite old. The Tromo Trochi of Dhomu approached, alternately sticking out his tongue and hissing at us, marks of good manners and proper etiquette. Sticking out the tongue is a customary way to say hello in this land that might surprise the average American. We were welcomed in this manner more than once.

As we offered to shake hands in our customary manner of saying hello he passed a white silk scarf, or kata, over our outstretched arms.

Lowell was very impressed with yaks as beasts of burden in Tibet.

We presented him with a similar scarf we brought from Sikkim. We shared tea and he hissed in approval of what he heard from his English translator. The agent bestowed an unusual honor upon us by inscribing some Tibetan characters on our two American passports and stamping them with the ancient seal of the Lhasa government. We were then presented with a scroll which guaranteed our safe conduct as guests of the country if we were stopped by anyone and challenged. No one did. In a country like Tibet word of mouth precedes your arrival so people likely knew we were coming and were authorized to be there.

Later, we saw our first large herd of yak. What an animal! Although he moves slowly, and rarely covers more than nine miles a day, he carries heavy burdens and is unfalteringly steady-footed on the steepest and most dangerous trails. The porters were very good and they organized the loads well on mules and a couple of yaks. It varied as we went along.

Many nights we slept beside campfires in the tents we brought, but we also were able to stay in various communities where the sirdar knew someone. They were compensated for letting us use their facility.

In the Himalayas the snow surrounds you. At lower elevations there were a lot of stones beneath us, bluffs with rocky trails. It was all very impressive. You know you're passing some of the highest mountains in the world. It was as if everything was in slow motion. While we did have rain, it wasn't very cold, or else it would have turned to snow.

Slowly, but steadily, we made our way towards Lhasa. It rained almost every day. It took us twenty-eight days and it rained on twenty-seven of them, although not all day every day. We arrived in Phari, which at 14,700 feet boasted of having the world's highest post office, but it was also known in some quarters as the world's dirtiest town. The translation of *Phari* is "Hog Hill."

However, we received a warm welcome in Phari from Rimshi Doti, the district governor. He was an imposing man who stood nearly seven feet tall, the tallest person we met in Tibet. Rimshi Doti presented us with two white scarves and with a large sack of barley and butchered lamb.

We were obliged to stop in any small settlement that we passed through. It was not as if they had foreign company very often and we were the object of curiosity, something quite natural in a nation which almost universally banned foreigners. We visited a monastery in Gyantse and we experienced another exchange of silk scarves and were presented with more eggs.

Near the end of our trek we had to traverse a major river, the Brahmaputra. We rode in comfort in skin boats. They were made of yak skin stretched taut over a framework of willow ribs. The boatmen, called kobos, sang as they rowed us and our baggage. Later, Dad was told that his description of the boat trip, combined with the kobos' singing, was one of his most popular broadcasts from Tibet. The river led us on our final push to Lhasa at a speed of about ten miles an hour.

Lowell Thomas Sr. receiving scarves as a welcome to Tibet from Rimshi Doti, a man seven feet tall, as he and Lowell Jr. approached Lhasa on their 1949 journey.

At last we reached Tibetan Highway Number One. Don't be fooled by the fancy name, however. This highway was not to be confused with a paved major highway in the United States. Where it was not completely submerged, it was a narrow trail through the rock. But it was here that we caught our first glimpse of Lhasa, the forbidden city, sparkling in the sunset, the Potala Palace standing out above the city, its golden roofs beckoning like a far-off beacon.

The entirety of the journey was like being in another world. It was a real adventure just getting there. We were under time pressure, as well. We didn't have unlimited time because the summer season is short and we wanted to get out before all of the surrounding mountain passes were shut down by winter snows. We had to keep an eye on the calendar. By October the monsoons would start and that was another thing you wanted to avoid getting caught by in the Himalayas. We had only just arrived and we had to keep track of how we spent our days because time would pass so swiftly in this magical country.

8

With the Dalai Lama in Lhasa

As honored guests of the country, Lowell and his father arrived in Lhasa, the Tibetan capital, on August 5, 1949, courtesy of the fourteenth Dalai Lama. Born Lhamo Thondup on July 6, 1935, the religious leader of the Tibetan people was discovered in the countryside and selected as the reincarnation of the thirteenth Dalai Lama two years after the passing of his predecessor and raised and educated to become the leader of his people when he turned fifteen in 1950. This Dalai Lama, who has resided in exile from Tibet for decades because Chinese Communists overran his homeland, has lived perhaps the most tumultuous, dramatic, pressure-filled, and episodic life of all the Dalai Lamas.

When the Thomases visited Tibet in 1949, the Dalai Lama was on the cusp of official manhood and was a year shy of being installed officially into his role as chief of the country. After a policy of exclusion of foreigners, the reason why this young Dalai Lama threw open the doors of Tibet to the Thomases was the same reason that ended up forcefully changing his own life. He was persuaded by a knowledgeable advisor that the threat of China taking over Tibet was a very real one and the Dalai Lama hoped that a fair hearing about the potential plight of the peace-loving and religious Tibetans would inspire Americans to come to their aid.

❖ ❖ ❖

LOWELL: The Tibetans decided to take a gamble and we were invited to Lhasa. The peril was imminent and the United States was virulently anti-Communist. The Communist radio had broadcast a number of times within recent months its plans to liberate Tibet. At the time of our visit only ten thousand Tibetan troops, armed with obsolete weapons, stood behind the mountain barrier to safeguard their homeland.

Our goal was to meet, talk with, photograph, and film the Dalai Lama. There was not much precedent for that. First, hardly any foreigners ever received approval to visit Tibet. Then it was out of the ordinary to obtain an audience with the Dalai Lama. There were many rules about what you were supposed to do if he engaged you in conversation. As for photography and filming, that was what we did professionally, but had no assurances before we reached Lhasa that the Dalai Lama would consent to be photographed. We did not know for sure when we reached Lhasa if the Dalai Lama would even meet with us. We didn't know, but we hoped for the best.

As we got closer to Lhasa one of the officials came out to greet us and escort us into the city. That person stayed with us as an interpreter as we went around the city to the monasteries. As you come upon the city there is a gate, an archway really, that is the entrance to the city. Of course the most striking thing is the Potala, the palace.

The huge palace was the home of the Dalai Lama and itself a symbol of Tibet and the peoples' love for Buddhism. Built in the middle seventeenth century, the Potala was placed on the UNESCO list of World Heritage structures in 1994. Situated atop a hill, the Potala consists of a white palace, which was the living quarters of the Dalai Lama, and the red palace in the center, completely devoted to Buddhist prayer and study. The structures dominate the landscape. Also quite impressive is the long staircase leading up from the city to the buildings well above sea level. It is most probable that photographs showing Lhasa will feature the Potala.

We gave up our tent living when we reached Lhasa. We were hospitably put up in the city. It was primitive by American standards, stone buildings with no central heating. It could have been much colder, especially at an altitude of more than eleven thousand feet, but it wasn't bad, and we were well-prepared. Nights were cool, but it was a warm time of year. It was still summer, even though we knew the weather could change quickly.

For sure, we were greeted by the people and officials warmly. They knew we had the blessing of the Dalai Lama and that we had the Dalai Lama's passport. So we were honored people, there officially. We hadn't sneaked across the border the way some explorers over past decades and centuries had tried to do. Sometimes those people had dressed as Tibetan coolies and tried to masquerade as locals, but they were always found out.

We were out-in-the-open Westerners when we went to the bazaar and mingled. We were a rare minority and we didn't look like anyone else there. We always had someone with us who was a Tibetan official wearing long red robes and so forth, so that was a signal that we were there officially, but that didn't mean the people weren't curious about us. Mostly, they smiled at us and that was all. They didn't generally try to ask questions. We were the ones who wanted to ask questions about everything. Later, we learned that at some point there was a Czechoslovakian Communist radio broadcast, apparently to support the Chinese, and it attacked my father as a spy because of our trip to Tibet. It stated, "An American expedition was sent to Tibet headed by an agent of the OSS (the Office of Strategic Services, the forerunner of the CIA), who modestly calls himself a radio commentator."

LOWELL SR. (memoir): The Kremlin weekly, *New Times*, attacked us on the grounds that we had been sent to Tibet to alienate it from China and turn it into an American colony. I must confess to being flattered. For what a secret agent I was. Not only did I neglect to consult with anyone in Washington about the trip—not even my old classmate Allen Dulles—I even forgot to take a letter or a gift to the Dalai Lama from President Truman, the most common courtesy. And, of course, considering my regular broadcasts and the news coverage we got, the entire affair was conducted with all the secrecy of a World Series.

LOWELL: It was my impression that if you were a visitor to Lhasa, the first thing the Dalai Lama saw to was that you were taken around as a tourist and shown everything so that you had a better grasp of your surroundings. Of course I'm not really sure they had much of an established procedure since this type of thing didn't happen often obviously.

We were taken to some monasteries and then we went inside the Potala, the Dalai Lama's palace. It's so very impressive. I remember there was some gold on the roof of the Potala. The colors were bright in the sun and it was great for photography. I was very keen to take as many film pictures as I could with my 16-millimeter camera. I got some good material. When I got home I did put together a film for an illustrated lecture called "Out of This World: A Journey into Forbidden Tibet." I also wrote a book of almost the same name about our trip called *Out of This World: Across the Himalayas to Forbidden Tibet.*

My father had dreamed of visiting closed Tibet for thirty years and when the invitation came it seemed as if we had the opportunity to take a rocket to the moon. We looked at it as a sealed land of mystery.

It was clear once we reached Lhasa that one reason we had approached on horseback was that the entire country was without wheels. Never mind the idea of jet travel and an airplane, there were no trucks or cars, or even carts, nothing that moved via wheels. It seemed incredible that this remote nation was living like that as late as the middle of the twentieth century.

My father made his tape recordings, but he also managed to find a way to broadcast reports live on shortwave radio. I remember that very well because one night in my excitement to be part of this short-wave conversation I kind of stole the show. Before I left on the trip, Tay and I had discussed marriage and had pretty much agreed we were going to get married. But we had not yet even told our parents. On the radio we sent some hello messages to people and I got on and I said

The flagstone steps that climb to the Potala as they looked in 1949 before the Chinese took over Tibet and the Dalai Lama fled to India.

something out of the blue. I asked Tay to marry me on the shortwave. It came across as something like this addressed to Tay, "We have a message from Lowell Thomas Jr." And then they read the message which was, "Hello from Tibet. Hope you will join me on the next trip."

Since I hadn't told my family yet about my marriage plans, I was a little embarrassed. Someone heard this, of course, and telephoned Tay's house in Connecticut and called at dinner time and told her parents what they had heard on the shortwave radio. Apparently there was some telephoning between the Pryor's house and mine. Both Tay's father and mine already knew each other well from the Explorer's Club. Tay's brothers glommed onto the message and began teasing her. Walter Winchell picked up the item and ran it in his syndicated column. That made it a very open message. When I got back I had some explaining to do. Tay and I joke about it all the time. We call it an arranged marriage.

People who saw the film were quite taken with our hiking and traversing of such rocky territory. I made it clear we were huffing and puffing in the beginning before we became acclimated. I think I made some people fans of yaks. Without yaks there would have been no Tibet. That's how important they were as beasts of burden. More than that, though, so much of Tibet was at high altitude with no trees there was no wood to burn for fires, to cook with or to keep warm. Mostly it was yak dung that was burned.

It occurred to me that the Tibetans had been living their lives in almost the same way for a thousand years. The only thing I could think of that compared was the Eskimos who have been living in Alaska for ten thousand years and follow many of the same subsistence habits today. Whether it was trekking or riding our horses through the rocky highlands or staring at the Potala and observing the old-fashioned way of living, at times we could hardly believe we were on the same planet as the United States. It seemed as if Lhasa with the Dalai Lama and the Potala was the Buddhist equivalent of Rome with the Pope and the Vatican and St. Peter's of the Catholic world.

We were very pleased to find the Dalai Lama very engaging and open to our ideas of photography and filming. We were told later that

The Dalai Lama as he looked at age fourteen in 1949 after granting Lowell Thomas Sr. and Jr. permission to visit Tibet to try to tell the world of Tibet's plight if the Chinese invaded.

when we were informed we could take all the photos we needed that had never happened before.

When we first met the Dalai Lama it was a formal-type audience. He was a boy, just fourteen. He smiled at us, he seemed curious about us, but he didn't say anything. He was sitting on his throne, just smiling. He must have said something in his language, but I don't really remember what it was. Again, this was a formal setting. We were there with a few other pilgrims who had come from other parts of Tibet to see him.

Our turn came to approach him and we went up and kneeled down beneath the throne. He reached over with the end of his stick and tapped us on the heads with it, imparting his blessing. That was very nice. It was later on that we were able to get him to come outside to where we could take photos and 16-millimeter pictures. The palace was very dark and it would have been difficult to shoot with such limited light. We went out into the garden. I had a Rollex, a little still camera with a flash and I got some good pictures of him, and did use the flash.

Once we reached Lhasa we did not travel around anywhere else. This is what we had come to see beyond the trail. We didn't venture any closer to China. We spent our time wandering around, taking pictures and notes. Later we did two pieces for *Collier's* magazine and one for the *National Geographic*. Then I did the book and had the illustrated lecture. I think we did give them good press, told people how wonderful and innocent their life was, although it was primitive. They were independent and had their own government and just wanted to be left alone, but the Chinese were on the verge of coming in to take over. We were really able to get the story out—my dad primarily—over the radio. As soon as we returned to the United States too, we had contact with the State Department, which wanted to know our impressions of what we saw and what might happen.

The American government didn't want to see the Communists take over Tibet, but China was claiming that Tibet was really part of its territory and that the United States had no business there. Because of the remoteness of Tibet, the United States was not in any position to offer enough aid or protection that could hold off the Chinese. The State Department didn't really seem as if it wanted very much information from us. The attitude was that it was up to the Indian government to try to do something. India had just become independent from Great Britain and wasn't really in a position of strength to do anything. Meanwhile, the Thomases went around telling the story of Tibet with radio reports and illustrated lectures and the written word. I gave a lecture on Tibet for several years, traveling all around the country and Canada too, telling the story, and it went over in a big way, but what it amounted to was just a travel adventure. There seemed to be a general sympathy towards Tibet then and which continues even now amongst the American people, but that hasn't made any kind of tangible difference in terms of preventing the Chinese government from doing what it wanted to do.

This photo of Lowell Jr. (left) and Lowell Sr. extreme right, with Tibetan religious figures, was snapped by famed mountaineer Heinrich Harrer in 1949 when they were all in Lhasa and given to Lowell Jr. as a gift. A copy still hangs in the Thomases' home in Anchorage.

Being the only other foreigners in Lhasa, it was natural that we would also meet Heinrich Harrer and Peter Aufschnaiter. Later, in the 1950s, I was surprised to realize that Harrer came to Alaska and made first ascents of some well-known mountains, Mount Deborah and Mount Hunter in the Alaska Range. They had been in Tibet for quite some time by then. Judging from the name of his book, Harrer was in Tibet for seven years altogether before he returned to Europe. Basically, after they escaped from the British prison camp they were granted asylum in Tibet. Again, that was something extremely out of the ordinary. Aufschnaiter had some very useful areas of expertise, being an engineer, and he had a working knowledge of the language. Harrer was pretty much a young climber, but against the odds he became a tutor and close friend of the Dalai Lama and they remained friends for the rest of Harrer's life.

We saw them off-and-on the whole time we were in Lhasa, several days, and had talks and visited. Theirs was a tremendously interesting story. How they managed to get there overland was really something. We had just experienced the difficulty of reaching Lhasa, escorted, on horseback, with the government stamp of approval. They were on foot, on the run, trying not to be recaptured and be returned as prisoners of war, and they had no government approval to be there, until after their case was pleaded in Lhasa. They had bandits along the way trying to rob them. We didn't experience anything like that. We were official visitors, so we were sort of in the "Don't touch" category as far as the bad guys went. We had a Tibetan corporal with us, riding with us the whole way, and I think he had a rifle.

When we were in Lhasa, Harrer and Aufschnaiter wore purple robes, ate Tibetan food, and spoke the language like natives. The Tibetans were fond of them. They, in turn, liked the Tibetans. It seemed to be a satisfactory combination. When we left Lhasa, Harrer and Aufschnaiter were on hand to bid us good-bye. We asked them whether they would not like to join us and return to their homeland and families. They declined. It was my impression at the time that they would probably stay in Tibet for the rest of their lives. That all changed when the Chinese arrived in force.

As late as May of 1950, I received a cheerful note from Aufschnaiter explaining his current project in Tibet. But before the year was over, the Chinese were making life very difficult for the Dalai Lama. Harrer's book *Seven Years in Tibet* sold three million copies in the 1950s. Much later, Aufschnaiter wrote his memoirs, which he titled *Eight Years in Tibet*, because before moving on to Nepal he stayed within the borders of the country ten months longer than Harrer.

In terms of the timing of being in Tibet, it was an intriguing intersection of history. The Dalai Lama, Harrer and Aufschnaiter, and two Lowell Thomases all there at the same time, just before the invasion of the Chinese army.

9

Life Threatening Challenges
on the Tibetan Trail

Before the Thomases departed the Tibetans could not have known that their efforts to tell the country's story to the world would be well-received yet generate no tangible help to prevent China from completing its mission. Both Lowell and his father loved their journey and to this day Lowell Jr. has souvenir photographs decorating walls of his Alaska home that recall that special trip to Tibet.

When the father and son team returned to the United States Lowell Jr. wrote the book about their expedition and created an illustrated lecture. Then he expanded the lecture film into a much more in-depth film about Tibet and it gained wide viewership. Lowell Sr. touched on Tibet in radio broadcasts and newsreels and he wrote about the adventure in the second volume of his memoirs.

The Dalai Lama saw his guests leave with hope in his heart that what they wrote and said would help convince the United States to aid his country and prevent it from falling into Communist hands. It did not, and as feared, the Chinese sent troops to Tibet and easily overpowered the small, ill-equipped guards of the Buddhist stronghold.

Throughout the 1950s the Dalai Lama coped with military regulations imposed from Beijing, but in 1959, during a Tibetan revolt, it became apparent that his life was probably in jeopardy if he

remained in Lhasa. The fourteenth Dalai Lama chose exile and dar-
ingly escaped Tibet and sought protection in India. For more than
fifty years the Dalai Lama has lived in exile, based in Dharamshala,
India, but has traveled the world seeking to keep the spotlight on the
plight of his country. At all times the religious leader acts as advocate for Tibetans living in Tibet as well as those who relocated outside the country since Chinese rule was imposed. In 1989, the Dalai
Lama was awarded the Nobel Peace Prize.

When their visit to Lhasa was complete, Lowell and his father
had to retrace their path back to India by the same route for three
hundred miles, using the same method of travel, and with the same
type of personnel for help. What had been a sterling adventure to
that point, however, nearly turned tragic. Lowell Sr. had a serious
accident that both he and his son wrote about in their respective
books and the consequences were life threatening.

Also, while they could not know what fate had in store for
Tibet, the ominous warnings in the atmosphere from the Chinese
government hinted at not only this being a once-in-a-lifetime trip,
but quite possibly the only time they would ever cross paths with the
Dalai Lama. As it so happened, the first was true. Tibet's doors were
again closed to anyone named Lowell Thomas, but for different reasons—the Communist regime's power. However, the latter proved
not to be true. Lowell Thomas Jr. did once again meet up with the
Dalai Lama, many years and many miles in the future.

❖ ❖ ❖

LOWELL: We had to beat the monsoon and the winter weather so we
couldn't stay in Lhasa indefinitely. We figured that it would take us at
least three weeks to trek back to India and Gangtok, though we were
going to be declining in altitude.

Our days passed swiftly and again the business of organizing a
caravan was our most pressing problem. Because Tibetans are supersti-
tious we had to leave on a lucky day—Monday, Wednesday, or Sunday.
Although we left Lhasa on a day of good omen we failed to dodge the

jinx which seems to haunt nearly every caravan of foreigners venturing into the mystical realm of the Dalai Lama.

It was on our retreat from Tibet that our adventure turned to misadventure. My father was climbing onto his horse, the horse swirled, and it dumped him on the ground. He was in a great deal of pain and we were not certain what the injury was, but suspected from the beginning he had broken his hip.

LOWELL SR. (memoir): Having dismounted to pick up some unusual colored rocks, I foolishly neglected to have anyone hold my unbroken horse's head when I started to mount him. That was the chance my steed—or the demon—was waiting for. Catching me with one foot in the stirrup and the other raised over the saddle the horse spun and sent me flying over the edge of the trail.

LOWELL: We had no doctor with us and only a limited first aid kit. We were really in the middle of nowhere and hundreds of miles from the closest city with modern medicine. This was a very, very bad location to have this kind of accident. We were in the mountains, in the Himalayas, probably at about fifteen thousand feet, maybe sixteen thousand feet. We stopped right where we were and made camp for a couple of days. We had to figure out what to do, but we were in a hard place and there weren't many solutions. My dad was in a great deal of pain and couldn't really move on his own. Initially, we didn't even have our first aid kit with us. It was traveling separately in our supply caravan miles behind, though it eventually caught up to us.

LOWELL SR: I felt the agonizing sensation of bones breaking in my hip as I came crashing down on the sharp rocks below. Almost at once I was struggling for breath in the thin air, struggling for consciousness. And even through the pain I knew that in such a desolate place there might be little I, or anyone, could do to stave off an abrupt end to all my years of travel. Heaven alone knew how long we would have to go to find medical help.

LOWELL: It was a challenging puzzle and a risky situation. We were very much in the wild and very much on our own at that moment. I stabilized my father the best I could and treated him with whatever medication we had in the first aid kit, though it wasn't much. There was no morphine and Dad was slipping into shock because of his agony.

LOWELL SR.: Lowell was holding me in his arms, which helped to keep my other bones from breaking apart as I shook with the chills and fever that at high altitude come swiftly with shock and exposure.

LOWELL: We wrapped him in a sleeping bag. The next move was to transform one of the canvas cots we had carried to sleep on into a stretcher and we hired some of the local guys to carry it and started moving again. We were going very, very slowly.

Moving was very tough. Dad was in excruciating pain and the pathway was neither level nor smooth. It was very rough trail. That first night after my father's injury it took six peasants and I to carry his litter and we reached shelter well after dark so he could rest indoors.

Although we were now inside, it was a terrible night for my father, one of the worst of his life. The shock and exposure brought on high fever and frequent fainting. His shattered hip gave him the very devil. No position was comfortable. Sleep was impossible. It was a long, gasping night of agony and worry in just about the most out-of-the-way spot you can find on this planet. Imagine being stricken in a land where the people don't believe in doctors, relying on the Lamas to cure ills through herbs, incantations, and ceremony.

We sent word about what happened down the trail by porter who reached the Indian agent in Gangtok representing the Indian government. They sent somebody out to assist us, but they couldn't do very much either. Next morning, Tsewong (the interpreter) and I hiked to the Ralung Monastery telephone. I prayed that the line was not down and that the Indian army doctor at Gyantse could come to the rescue. It was almost a matter of life or death. Without a doctor to splint Dad's leg I could see no way to ever get him home. Though Gyantse was only

After Lowell Thomas Sr. was tossed by his horse and injured in the wilderness of Tibet in 1949, he could not walk because of what was believed to be a broken leg and hip. A throne-like chair was rigged to carry him and porters traded off the duty.

thirty-three miles away, to join us the doctor needed special permission granted by the Tibetan government. The Tibetan trade agent gave the nod and the good doctor, one of only four in Tibet, made a forced march in one day.

The doctor did not have the ability to do an X-ray—there was no X-ray machine in Tibet—but he suggested it was possible that Dad's injury might only be muscular, torn ligaments. We decided to press on to Gyantse as best we could. It sometimes took ten Tibetans to carry Dad's stretcher over the steep, rocky trails, which skirted chasms and swift streams, moving at a snail's pace. Strapped to the stretcher, leg in a splint, Dad roasted when the sun was out and nearly froze when it ducked behind the clouds and the cold winds blew up. On the third day we reached Gyantse.

We spent ten days at the Indian garrison and with rest and

provisions Dad felt better. He somehow managed to begin walking the twenty yards to the mess hall with the aid of a cane. This effort fooled us into concluding that the hip or leg was not broken. I think it was sheer willpower and guts that enabled him to walk on that limb.

LOWELL SR.: But both Lowell and I knew the worst was still ahead of us.

LOWELL: By slowing down and lingering in Gyantse, we were tempting fate, as well, with the weather. What we really needed was for a plane to airlift Dad out of there and to somewhere he could obtain more sophisticated medical care before we were trapped by the snows. If unlucky, we could be marooned there until the summer of 1950. Obtaining a plane was impossible. We had to push on and we fashioned our own magic carpet for Dad. We used a stout wooden sedan chair as his throne and he was carried on the shoulders of Tibetans. When I say stout it was estimated that the chair alone weighed 150 pounds. Two weeks had passed since the calamity with the horse before we moved back onto the trail. It was a long trail too. It took us another sixteen days to cover the two hundred or more miles remaining from Gyantse to Gangtok.

Tibetans carried Dad's chair in rotating groups of four and they switched off every half hour. Bounce, bounce, bounce, hour after hour, day after day. We were also fortunate to have a medical man join us periodically to make end-of-the-day checkups of my father after being on the trail for ten hours at a stretch. Somewhat regularly, the porters sang the same song. When I asked for its translation I was told the words meant, "O, Lord Buddha, lighten our load." The prayer was answered too, for on that journey Dad lost twenty pounds.

We saw the same magnificent scenery on the trip out of Tibet as we had on the way in, but it didn't seem to make as much of an impact. There were other things on our mind and we were worried about my father's health. As the days dragged by we thought we'd never make it.

While he was riding in that chair my father was in good spirits. Maybe he was that way because of what the other medical person had said about the injury only being torn ligaments or muscular.

LOWELL SR.: Young Lowell, without whose resourcefulness and determination to get me out alive I could never have made it. . . .

LOWELL: On October 5 we were met by a rescue team sent out by Loy Henderson, United States Ambassador at New Delhi, with the cooperation of the Indian government. As if the rescue team was not enough, the United States Air Force ordered a plane to the nearest airfield to help with our evacuation. At Siliguri, just south of Gangtok, the American air attaché to India picked us up in his C-47 and flew us on to Calcutta. From there to America it was no problem.

   Once home, no time was wasted getting Dad to a hospital in New York where his leg was operated on successfully. His right hip and leg, which had begun to knit improperly during the month since the accident, were re-broken and properly set. Closely examined by more experienced doctors with more sophisticated equipment, the diagnosis was that Dad had broken his leg in eight places. It was definitely not a torn ligament and it was inconceivable that he was walking on it at Gyantse.

   For more than six months Dad needed crutches to aid his walking. But less than a year later he was able to take a ski trip to Alaska outside of Juneau.

   After Dad was taken to the hospital, I was anointed as the spokesman for the trip in a visit to the White House to see President Harry Truman. I delivered a scroll from Tibet to the president. The message had been handwritten in Tibetan characters with a bamboo pen on parchment made from the bark of a Tibetan tree. The Tibetan officials were right to worry. It was not long before the Chinese arrived in their corner of the world in full force and changed their way of life.

   When the president asked about our journey I opened a map for him and traced the route we had followed. President Truman surprised me when he said he had long dreamed of visiting Lhasa. After looking at the map and hearing the tale of our route, though, he said he probably would never have the opportunity.

LOWELL SR.: Some months later, still on crutches, I also went to Washington to pay my respects to the president and Secretary of State Dean Acheson. Dean Acheson listened to me tell about our trip across the Himalayas, but gave no indication it might be possible for America to help the Tibetans. President Truman not only gave me an hour or more…he also took me over to a globe and showed me where he said we were going to contain Communists in Asia. He also had no promise of any help for the Dalai Lama and his people.

LOWELL: As the years have passed, and after the Dalai Lama went into exile in the face of the Chinese aggression, I have often read newspaper stories or seen television accounts of his doings. Never do I read his name in print or see his face without thinking of our meeting with him in Tibet and the glorious trip my father and I took to the forbidden country.

Decades later in the United States, New York or Washington, I am not sure, my father and I saw the Dalai Lama again. He was well into adulthood then. We shook hands and we bowed and he bowed and then in English he said to us, "Like another life." It was a remarkably simple and direct acknowledgment of our meeting in Tibet so long before. That really did say a lot in one sentence. "Like another life." I always remember him saying that. It was like a lifetime had passed between our meetings and so much had happened in the world in the intervening years. It was very powerful and very accurate.

I have thought of my journey to Tibet in that way too. I was only twenty-five and so much time has passed.

10

Two Lifetime Passions: Tay and Flying

Lowell Thomas Jr.'s interest in flying and becoming a pilot was ingrained in him at a young age. He gained the knowledge needed to become a pilot while serving in the Army Air Corps during World War II. But once he was discharged from the service it was not readily apparent how he would be able to maintain his ability to fly. He did not own an airplane and he did not have a job working for an airline.

In the late 1940s, Thomas was busy making films, going off to Tibet, working as an advance scout on films for his father, taking graduate courses at Princeton. But he hadn't forgotten about flying. He was just looking for a way in to become a pilot.

Once, after Lowell and Tay were getting serious about their relationship, Lowell borrowed a small plane from a friend to fly it to Northampton, Massachusetts, where she was enrolled, just for a weekend visit. Most guys drive to their girlfriends' colleges for short visits.

Lowell always sought opportunities to fly. He remained under the sway of his early-in-life impressions made by such great American pilots as Jimmy Doolittle and Eddie Rickenbacker. He could always recall the stories they told his father and their dramatic lives were part of the background whenever Thomas thought about a life's work in aviation.

Just as youngsters growing up in the United States in the 1960s might have been motivated to become astronauts because of all the attention thrown on the nation's space program, Thomas was born in the 1920s when aviation was just beginning to assert its grip on the American public. He grew up simultaneously to the expansion of aviation as an industry, and looked at through another lens, of aviation as a romantic pursuit.

❖ ❖ ❖

LOWELL: Aviation was just one of those things that kids latched onto during that time period. Before that, I suppose it was trains and railroads for another generation of kids. For me aviation was a big thing. I was just captivated by the story of aviation. Before I joined the Air Corps I did a little bit of flying with a friend who owned an airplane. I'd go with him and hold the wheel a little bit.

Mostly, I was a passenger, but once in a while I guided the plane. When I got into the Air Corps and got my wings and commission and became an instructor, that's when I really learned to fly. After the war I was interested in flying in a civilian capacity. Whenever I got the chance to borrow an airplane and take a flight I would do it. There was a little air coupe around that was designed to be a plane that you couldn't spin. It didn't have all of the full controls of most planes, but at least it got me up into the air. I borrowed the air coupe for the flight to go visit Tay in Northampton, Massachusetts. It wasn't too long after I got back from Tibet and Tay graduated from Smith College that we got married in Christ Episcopal Church in Greenwich, Connecticut. The church was packed with many of our parents' well-known friends so there were pictures in the newspapers afterward, but Tay and I paid little attention to that.

After my dad and I got back from Tibet I wrote the book about the trip and put together a film to give illustrated adventures. Once that was ready, and after Tay and I were married in May of 1950, we went on the road together when I was speaking. We took the train most of the time, but we flew sometimes when it was possible.

It was in the early fifties that I got my first airplane. It was a Stinson Voyager. It was a high-winged plane and I found it for sale at the airport near Greenwich. I went to take a look, flew it a little bit, and we decided to get it. It probably cost four thousand or five thousand dollars. It was a single-engine plane with four seats.

You had the pilot and the seat next to him and the back was a sling seat. You could fit a couple of more people in there or you could take the seat out and use it for baggage. It was not a plane that you could fly very fast. I think the maximum you could go was about ninety miles per hour.

We were living in Princeton, New Jersey. I had enrolled in the graduate school there, still with the US Foreign Service in the back of my mind, but I never did finish there, or try to join the Foreign Service. We had the plane with us and we used it quite often going from our home to a log cabin near my family's property where I had grown up in Pawling, New York. We could fly there in an hour and fifteen minutes, as opposed to a three-hour drive, when the weather was good. Bringing the plane in for a landing I don't think it was going any faster than fifty or fifty-five miles an hour.

Other times we flew to Greenwich to visit Tay's family and just to use it for our own transportation instead of going another way to get somewhere. When the weather was good and we had time so that we knew we would get there in advance and not be delayed, we flew the plane to someplace where I was scheduled to give one of my illustrated lectures on Tibet. Sometimes we would go a day early just to spend time in the community. We didn't fly very often because of the threat of bad weather forcing us down and wrecking our schedule. I knew that if I didn't get there, there would be hell to pay.

Once the Tibet film was ready, I was very busy with lectures. Everyone wanted to hear it. Right after we were married it was very popular and we went all over the country and to Canada all of that following winter.

TAY: Ours was a working honeymoon. We flew to Hawaii and paid for it by giving one lecture to over four thousand people in an overflowing auditorium. Later, we flew all around the western part of the country while Lowell was an advance man for Cinerama. I particularly remember flying down into the Grand Canyon at five o'clock in the morning, zooming low in our little plane. Of course, the Park Service doesn't allow anyone to do that anymore. But it was a great thrill because I had never seen it. Then we went to Zion and Bryce Canyon in Utah and they are beautiful from a low altitude. That was a summer to remember.

LOWELL: We were flying all of the time on those trips in the west, but on all of the short trips to our Pawling cabin, Tay's family home, to cities where I lectured. I was able to build up flight time and experience in the cockpit. I certainly didn't need all of the information I learned in the Air Force since I was only flying single-engine planes, but I did have a good background with instruments from my military flying. We did a little bit of that even in single-engine planes in fairly good weather, just to practice.

TAY: We got to go to Rio de Janeiro when Lowell was the advance man for Cinerama, although we flew commercial. In fact, we traveled over most of Africa and the Middle East all the way to Burma and Thailand. That's when we got to thinking, "Oh, wouldn't it be fun if we could just do this without landing in the cities and flying commercially?" We started talking about flying off the beaten path in a little plane of our own and that's what built up to our 1954 trip, the flight to adventure.

LOWELL: After a while of doing all this flying to cities where we had to go for business, Tay and I got to a stage in our lives when we wanted to go off by ourselves and see faraway places, do it in our own way, and even do it in our own airplane.

Tay and I were young and we weren't tied down and we didn't have any children at the time. This would be a kind of second honeymoon trip. It was a big responsibility in the sense that I would have to do all of the flying with Tay as the navigator and it would be a big undertaking to plan.

TAY: I said I would love to go on such a trip around the world, but I won't fly across the Atlantic in a small plane. That's how we ended up starting from Paris. We went and talked to Charles Lindbergh about flying the Atlantic since, of course, he was the first one to do it in 1927, and he told us, "I think that you really should avoid flying over a large amount of water in a single-engine plane."

LOWELL: I didn't really want to fly across the Atlantic in a small plane either. What we were aware of from the start was being sharp on the logistical planning. We wanted to go to places where almost no one went. Certainly there was no tourism industry in the places we were hoping to visit. Not in the early 1950s, right after World War II. I wasn't concerned about flying. I was worried about the hassles of red tape when arriving in these out-of-the-way countries that didn't expect visitors.

During that time period, Americans wanted to hop on a jet, fly across the Atlantic Ocean, and visit London or Paris, but Tay and I had bigger plans than that. We wanted to take our own plane where other planes did not generally fly. It was unusual for anyone to show up in many countries in their own private airplane. It would make a hubbub and when you are thousands of miles from home you want things to go smoothly. We had to work through our State Department and foreign embassies to set our arrivals in advance. We had to work very carefully to make sure we had paperwork that was in order so, preferably, when we landed somewhere everything would be OK. We couldn't just take off and go someplace without anybody knowing where we were going or why, even if we would have liked to do that. It definitely took a little bit of diplomacy to get that all worked out.

Another critical aspect of the advance planning was having an understanding of the fuel situation everywhere we were going and where we would be able to obtain it. It doesn't do you any good to try to fly around the world if you can't get enough gas to fly around the world. Contemplating the trip led us to decide we needed a bigger and faster plane than the Stinson Voyager. We kept thinking about Africa and the Middle East and what the conditions would be. We needed a plane with better takeoff performance, more carrying capacity and range.

I made a trip to the manufacturing plant in Wichita, Kansas, where they made the Cessna 180. The idea was to eventually turn it over to the Cessna Company of Australia. We were delivering it, with a few stops in between. I got the plane on a letter of credit. When we got to Australia they were supposed to take the plane off our hands and it wouldn't have cost us anything except the insurance and the transportation costs of getting it across the ocean. It was a pretty good deal. That was the original plan, only we never made it to Australia and we decided to keep the plane. All of these years later it is still flying, even if I am not. We brought the plane home. The tail number is 2343C (I promptly named it *Charlie* for that reason) and it's still around, still going. That says something for the workmanship. I don't know how many automobiles are still on the road from 1954. Not many, I'll bet. The Cessna 180 was a great plane and I loved it.

It was our aim to fly far from the beaten path wherever that was possible. We hoped to meet and spend a good deal of time among some of the world's more remote peoples. We wanted to learn what we could about them, and having done so, to make some kind of a report of our findings in the belief that the more knowledge there is of other peoples and other lands, the less misunderstanding there will be and the greater chance for international cooperation and world peace.

To avoid flying across the Atlantic Ocean in a small plane we had the Cessna disassembled and shipped to France ahead of us. *Charlie* was waiting for us by the time Tay and I left New York on the ship the SS *America* on February 22, 1954, to rendezvous with the plane.

Once we left the harbor we found our stateroom. We loaded it with two suitcases and piles of boxes containing camera and sound gear, airplane spare parts, and a duffle bag of camping supplies. While Tay

Lowell with the disassembled Cessna 180 that he flew 50,000 miles in with Tay in 1954 and 1955 through Europe and Africa.

attempted to make things more orderly I went back on deck to watch the New York shoreline gradually disappear. Tay and I were on our own. We were now freelance writers and photographers planning to record our travels. We already had a signed contract with Doubleday Publishers.

The Cessna company had people in France at the Toussus-le-Noble Airfield outside Versailles, where *Charlie* was reassembled and waiting for us. We thought we could make a good story for a company that helped us out so much. The first airplane manufacturer we had approached for support said it didn't want to have anything to do with us because it would be bad publicity if we crashed and died. Cessna had a lot better attitude about our trip.

We took a test flight immediately. Off to the north were the crowded rooftops of Paris, with the Eiffel Tower standing tall and slender against the horizon some eight or nine miles away, and with the Seine River looping back and forth through the city and across the countryside. But when it was time to go, our course lay in the opposite direction, to Spain and on to Africa.

Before we could depart, however, there was one minor obstacle. We had brought thirty pieces of luggage with us for our planned year away from home and there was not nearly enough room to accommodate them inside *Charlie*. We decided to send home all of our dress clothing. Tay shipped home her golden slippers and admitted, "A little more emergency water will be worth far more over the Sahara Desert."

TAY: Actually, when we were talking to Charles Lindbergh, he gave us a very good tip. He said, "I would suggest that when you fly over desert areas if you carry water bottles, they should be hot water bags." That's what he called them. Not canteens. They were rubber. They were very unusual. I'd never heard of anybody talk about water bottles like that before. He said, "Carry six hot water bags and keep them empty when you're flying over places where you will always find water. But when you go over the desert you can fill them up and keep them on the bottom of the plane. His thought was that hot water bottles were not as breakable as glass and would take up less room when empty.

LOWELL: Out went a thermos jug and a spare flashlight, a carton of books too, and even Mae West life vests. It is surprising how many absolutely essential belongings aren't essential at all when one has to get rid of them. Larger and larger grew our pile of discards. Smaller and smaller grew the load we hoped to make *Charlie* carry. Finally our total load amounted to 525 pounds, which was 250 pounds more than the civilian aviation authorities had licensed the plane to carry. We decided not an ounce more could go.

That did not apply to the one-ounce piece of paper that Tay pasted on the instrument panel. We never did find out who wrote the poem, but we carried it throughout every mile of the aerial journey. It read:

"Peace be in thy home,
And in thy heart,
Or if thou roam Earth's highways wide,
The Lord be at thy side To bless and guide."

Months and months of preparation and really, years of thought wrestling with the idea had passed, but the day finally arrived when we taxied down the runaway outside of Paris, headed for a year of adventure, the plane pointed to Gibraltar.

11

Around the World

L owell and Tay Thomas were on a dream trip. It was the type of journey that people pine for, imagine, fantasize about, talk about, and yet practically never make because daily life interferes, it costs too much, or something weds them to home. They were wed to each other and didn't worry about much else.

Even sixty years later, duplicating such a trip would be viewed as dramatically bold. Political pressures, changes in geographical boundaries, and additional government red tape would probably intervene and prevent it from being accomplished in the same manner as the couple pulled it off. Very likely someone flying his own plane as Lowell did would be frowned upon by authorities in various countries. If a couple attempted today to do exactly what Lowell and Tay achieved, skeptics ahead of time would probably say, "Good luck, you'll need it."

It was the Thomases' intention to travel for at least a year and essentially make a circuit around the world. They had a general schedule and some stopping points that were a must-see, but were not rigidly bound by their plan, so they could stick around someplace if they found it pleasant.

A year is a whopping long adventure, but a year is not really enough time to see the entire world either. Lowell and Tay planned to do the best they could before returning to the United States sometime in 1955.

They departed France with a sense of excitement and a taste for the unknown. They were headed to some places where few Westerners had been and to some places that were in the most remote of locations. Basically, they were on their own with *Charlie* their airplane, except in some cases where strangers had been alerted they might drop in from the sky to visit.

◆ ◆ ◆

LOWELL: After all of the planning and organizing, when we took off in France it was a very liberating feeling. Tay immediately said, "Can you believe that we're really on our way?" That summed up our emotions. We were up in the air. We were flying. Our long-awaited trip had begun.

Several villages on the Orleans Railway appeared one after another below us, but the polished rails turned toward the south after fifty miles or so while we continued on our course. We headed toward the chateau country of the Loire at 150 miles an hour. We hadn't yet settled into our routine and Tay, the navigator, was looking around at the scenery.

TAY: We headed down the coast and it felt like, "Gee, we're free. We're doing this by ourselves." It was just wonderful. It was fun. We could go wherever we wanted to and land and spend the night, or maybe two or three nights. We just didn't lock ourselves into a schedule. And when we felt we had enough material to write, we would find a nice place where we could set down and spend a few days and write or film. We went down the coast of Spain and I remember that very well because the weather turned bad and I got a little nervous. There was rain and poor visibility.

One of the first thrills we had was seeing Mont-Saint-Michel in France. It was a little castle in the middle of the ocean with just a little road connection which disappeared at high tide. The whole island is only 247 acres and the highest point is only three hundred feet above sea level. Practically no one lives there. I guess now they have improved their connections to the mainland and they do have a real road. Actually, this "little castle" is now on UNESCO's World Heritage Sites list, and so is the bay around it. More than three million people a year visit it.

LOWELL: We received a report that Barcelona had a ceiling of two thousand feet and visibility of ten miles. This was good news. But later we ran into a low mat of gray clouds that forced us down to seven hundred feet and rain began to ping against the windshield. According to the report we had just received Barcelona's weather was confidently saying, "Come on. Come on. You can make it." But the low clouds and rain were sounding a warning. Our policy, which we sometimes found difficult to follow, was to stay out of any overcast or other blind flying conditions.

We began to regret having chosen this route. There was no area of farm land. There was no level land at all—not even any beaches. The Mediterranean was pounding with frothy fists against abrupt and barren cliffs behind which, on our right, the broken terrain rose steeply, disappearing almost at once into the clouds. I was forcefully reminded of some advice Charles Lindbergh had given us. In a single-engine plane, he said, we should avoid flying over any terrain where we could not land.

I looked down at the rocks and cliffs below and considered the disconcerting fact that *Charlie's* minimum power of landing speed was about fifty-five miles an hour. I naturally wondered just how we would fare if we should be forced to land among those rocks and boulders at any such speed.

For quite a while our windshield had been growing harder to see through and at last I learned why. I was careful not to tell Tay, but I had to admit to myself that the rain on the windshield was mixed with engine oil. In another fifteen minutes, cliffs and rocks began to give way to a narrow ribbon of beach which soon came to be flanked by green fields. The weather improved too, as the coastline curved sharply toward Barcelona. Now there were plenty of places for a forced landing. Still, our 225 horsepower Continental engine was purring contentedly, as if a little thing like an oil leak made no difference. I suppose there were times as a pilot when I got nervous, but I don't recall ever getting panicky. I knew what I was doing and remained confident.

We were five minutes out when we picked up the airport beacon. Only it wasn't Barcelona. It was a military field. We rolled onto the base with the throttle closed and let the air speed fall off to a hundred. The runway lights snapped on and in another moment *Charlie* was on the ground. As the propeller came to a rest, a group of soldiers appeared, marching toward us. Both Tay and I felt it advisable to arm ourselves with our friendliest smiles against the imminent arrival of this most businesslike welcoming committee. They turned out to be a detail of Francisco Franco's military police, whose ankle-length coats, shiny boots, and large black holsters immediately stirred up memories of Hitler's SS. I said to Tay, "You took two years of Spanish." But she said they were talking too quickly for her to understand what they were saying.

TAY: I couldn't remember a single word. I just pointed to the map indicating that we were looking for the big airport. They sort of said, "Oh well," with big smiles.

LOWELL: A civilian who spoke English was ferreted out. We succeeded in answering their many questions about where we came from, where we were going, and why, and all sorts of questions about our plane. We never did find out just what they wanted. We ultimately decided that they merely wished to let us know that they were police. We figured that they thought we were just a couple of stupid, lost Americans. I think they laughed as they finally waved us off.

We got right back in the air and landed at the main airport [in Barcelona]. We headed downtown in an ancient yellow taxi cab. The Spanish Civil War took place before World War II began, but that taxi was surely a survivor—and possibly an actual veteran. We had intended to take off in the morning, but rain and fog decided otherwise and socked us in for three days.

That gave us time for *Charlie* to have a thorough going over. Desmond Drea was the head American mechanic for Pan American there and he looked everything over carefully. The diagnosis of the oil leak was that perhaps the crankcase had just been too full.

We hoped to reach Gibraltar in a single hop, but rain was falling. Our plan was to move in as close as conditions allowed. We were still fifteen miles from Cartagena and the map we had before us was anything but strong in its details. Still, it showed us what seemed to be the only airfield anywhere near the city. We landed on the runway going away from the hangars and other airport buildings, and as we taxied back a jeep full of soldiers roared out to the runway's end to intercept us.

The soldiers piled out of their jeep and I quite consciously put on my very best smile. "Hi," I began. "This is Cartagena, isn't it?" Stony silence followed. Tay was alert and broke the tension by handing me the map. The commander began to explain to us in broken English that we had the wrong field. "You—finding Carmelli," he said. That's where he sent us. Tay commented that we were lucky to get out of that fix so easily. In less than half an hour we were over Alicante. There was the airfield too, but just as we were all set to drop down we spotted a row of barracks and platoons of marching soldiers. "Oho!" we thought, "another military field. Better not tempt fate twice."

We backtracked to Valencia and rain followed us, keeping us there an extra day. Finally, we burst through the last shower of rain into welcome sunshine. We had Gibraltar in our sights at last.

I rolled *Charlie* into a long, gentle descent for Gibraltar 130 miles away. More for amusement than anything else, I flipped on our VHF radio and gave Gibraltar a call on their frequency. I had often found it impossible to contact Spanish stations sometimes when we were as close as ten miles. It is no wonder that Gibraltar's immediate reply surprised me.

We were over the coast at Málaga and there it was, the Rock of Gibraltar. What a thrill to see for the first time this world-renowned and unique landmark, this vast rock that was known to the ancient

Greeks as one of the Pillars of Hercules. It was an even greater thrill to land there, for at the time few private aircraft had ever done so. The tower operator told us later he had been surprised to learn that we had been given permission by the authorities in London.

Tay opened her window and aimed the motion picture camera at the Rock, which rears its naked summit 1,396 feet above the end of a long and narrow peninsula. Coming into Gibraltar can be tricky when the wind is not just right. Among our papers was a publication entitled "International Flight Information Manual," and it warned, "Do not fly near the Rock: Dangerous downdrafts and extreme turbulence, particularly on leeward side."

The Rock of Gibraltar is a British possession, even though it borders Spain, and there was a Royal Air Force station there when we arrived. The Moors occupied the Rock of Gibraltar for seven hundred years, starting soon after AD 700 and there is a ruin of a Moorish castle there. I read somewhere that during World War II there were as many as thirty thousand British airmen stationed on the Rock.

TAY: What I always remembered from reading about the Rock of Gibraltar were the monkeys. The monkeys are Barbary macaques and they are the only members of that species on the European continent. I had also read about the monkeys living in caves and hiding in the rocks all around the island.

LOWELL: We had not eaten since seven o'clock in the morning and we were extremely hungry. We felt certain we would be able to obtain some food at the R.A.F. canteen, but were seriously disappointed that we could find nothing edible but Cadbury chocolate bars and Coca-Cola. That is all we had for our belated lunch.

There was no plan to stay very long on the Rock of Gibraltar, as pleased to see it as we were, and we made ready to depart very quickly. We were leaving the Iberian Peninsula to fly onward to Africa, one of our main destinations. Tay, who dislikes flying over water, was all for crossing the Strait of Gibraltar by the shortest way, but that was out.

Getting *Charlie*, the Cessna, loaded for the flight to Africa.

There was a large prohibited area on the African coast and the only thing that seemed not to be a prohibited area was a single, narrow corridor that led from Spain to Spanish Morocco about midway along the strait.

So that is the way we went, hemmed in on both sides by imaginary lines beyond which we were not supposed to wander lest we bring down all sorts of official wrath upon our heads. But hardly more than fifteen minutes after taking off from Gibraltar we had left Europe behind and were hurrying across the African coastline.

Geographically there is little difference between the land we were flying over just ten miles from Spain and this new land, but it seemed much more fascinating and exciting. Here was Africa and the westernmost portion of the Mohammedan world, the land known to Arabs as "Land Farthest West."

Heading to Africa was one of our great objectives of this journey. Unlike France and Spain, we knew that we were heading to countries where the lifestyles and people were dramatically different from those we knew in the United States and met in Western Europe. For Tay and me Africa had great allure and was a place of great mystique.

12

Welcome to Africa:
The Western Desert and Timbuktu

In the early 1950s, many of the countries in Africa were still under colonial administration. England, Belgium, and France essentially controlled several nations, had a military presence, and were the de facto governments. That was soon to change as the continent moved dramatically and sometimes violently toward nationalism and one by one the African countries declared independence.

At the time, in the first years after World War II, countries Lowell and Tay visited were peaceful and the rumblings of the troubled times soon to come had not yet been felt. Africa was for the most part a Third World continent, still finding its way in the modern world. Technology and development trailed the United States and Western Europe by tremendous amounts.

It was still possible to mingle with inhabitants who lived completely different lifestyles than Americans were used to seeing. In many places there was no electricity or refrigeration. Lowell and Tay encountered people whose lives were still very much rooted in lifestyles of a century or even longer before. At the same time they were also tourists, seeing the magnificent sights and scenery of the world, some of which were acknowledged marvels and some of which they just saw for themselves and marveled at.

Foremost on Tay's mind was viewing the Rwenzori Mountains because she had studied and written about them while at Smith College. For ages, the source of the Nile River had eluded man's best attempts to pinpoint it. In 1858, British explorer John Hanning Speke became the first Westerner to see Lake Victoria while part of Richard Francis Burton's African expedition. Although the men later feuded over the discovery, it was proven that Speke had indeed uncovered the source of the Nile.

The goal of the two-person Thomas expedition was to see as much as possible that couldn't be seen at home and meet people who lived as differently from Americans as could be imagined. Africa was the place to do that.

❖ ❖ ❖

LOWELL: It didn't take long before the Rock of Gibraltar faded behind us. Our destination was Rabat, Morocco. We realized we were flying over the area that the ancients thought was the end of the world and passed over the Tangier International Zone from Spanish Morocco to French Morocco.

We followed the coastline devoid of landmarks that meant anything to us and then made our first landing in Africa at Rabat Ville. A Shell Oil representative gave us a ride into town and as we passed through an arch in the old city wall we caught a glimpse of white-robed Arabs with rifles slung over their shoulders. They were guards for the Sultan's palace. We were taken to the city's principal hotel, which was almost a palace in its own right with marble floors and towering pillars and frescoed ceilings. We visited the tourist bar before dinner, sitting on low couches while yellow-slippered, white-robed waiters with red fezzes on their heads served us. Tay whispered to me that she felt just like the Sultan's daughter in such an atmosphere.

We had hoped during our visit that we might be able to film Moulay Mohammed Ben Arafa, who was the new Sultan. But we had arrived at a most unfortunate time. Only the week before, one of the Sultan's disgruntled subjects had thrown a hand grenade at him. For the time being, at least, photography was out of the question.

Although we desired to stay around for a little while, the hotel had room for us for just one night. Tay and I had decided not to make reservations as we went so we would not be tied down to a schedule. This was one of the few times that proved to be a problem. So we left for Marrakech the next day. When we took off in Rabat, we flew over the Sultan's palace. Looking down directly into its private courtyards we even saw the royal laundry hanging up to dry.

It was only 150 miles from Rabat to Marrakech, but in between we saw the High Atlas Mountains, with altitudes to more than thirteen thousand feet and I detoured to the grand peaks where Tay opened the window and took pictures.

Deep in Morocco the region was pretty much unknown to Westerners until our time and we realized we had reached a tourist's paradise. Our hotel in Marrakech was luxuriously elegant with marble halls and a mammoth dining room with glass doors looking out at beautiful formal gardens. The warm climate, the semidesert vegetation, and the mountains in the distance all reminded me of Tucson, Arizona.

The square of Jemaa el-Fna—the Concourse of Sinners—stood at the very heart of Marrakech, in the old section of the city, and was one of the famous landmarks of Morocco. The great marketplace was lined with shops and orange trees. The people who were milling about everywhere formed a colorful and varied throng. White-robed, red-fezzed city dwellers mingled with country shepherds, turbaned farmers, hooded Berbers, and burnoosed Arabs, and here and there a resident Frenchman. Tay and I were most conspicuous in such a gathering. We soon found ourselves followed by an insistent little crowd. Groups of people were at our elbows wherever we turned, pulling at my sleeve or at Tay's skirt. I took a year of Arabic at Princeton, but it didn't do me much good here at the bazaar. Arabic is a tough language to learn.

TAY: We were much better off in the African countries that used French as a second language. Lowell would speak French and I would understand the French spoken back. I would translate and he would speak.

LOWELL: At the bazaar, we came upon a snake charmer, already surrounded by a throng. We were thrust up close to him and I thought he would be photogenic. He was a wild-eyed fellow, half crazed in appearance, with disheveled hair. He pranced about and rubbed the snake's head along the sides of his nose and chin. A time or two he popped the snake's head into his mouth. Two Berbers kept time on a couple of finger-tapped drums and a flute. As I aimed the camera the snake charmer grabbed Tay's wrist, waving the snake in front of her. She cried out in fright and did her best to pull away. The crowd laughed uproariously.

As we made our way through the Marrakech bazaar we often felt that the atmosphere was suspicious or unfriendly. Both of us were troubled now and again by the many pairs of eyes that followed us with apparent disapproval as we passed through some of the darker, narrower passageways.

Our thoughts turned to the Atlas Mountains and the skiing prospects. In a tiny French car we borrowed from the chief Shell man, we took the two-hour drive to a chalet where we were able to secure the use of poles and skis. We did not see many experts, but we saw many enthusiasts. While Tay found a pair of ski pants I had to settle for my khaki shorts. Upon seeing me one astonished Frenchwoman exclaimed, "Quelle horreur!"

It was an hour wait for either of the lift lines. The slopes were wide, fairly steep and completely treeless. Most of our fellow skiers were there merely for the day. Only the proprietor, his family, and another couple shared the chalet for dinner with us. Tay and I skied and photographed and soaked up the brilliant sunshine that flooded the Atlas for three days.

The loaner of our car had left with it, so when it was time to leave we called a taxi. However, the weather changed and a snowstorm developed. We soon were bogged down in a snow-filled ditch. Tay and I were about to start walking when a member of the French Foreign Legion at the end of a hike spotted us. He promised to send help from his barracks and did so. Our rescuers drove us to a run-down little restaurant two miles farther down the mountain where we found about a dozen others who were snowbound too. Ultimately we were transported back up the mountain to the chalet in a French Foreign Legion ambulance, apparently the only vehicle around with four-wheel drive. We were only stuck there overnight, however. The following day we reunited with *Charlie* and flew back to Rabat.

To our delight we received permission to land at and actually photograph the great airfield of Sidi Slimane, one of the US Strategic Air Command bases in Morocco. As we were attempting to come in for a landing we were surrounded by Sabre jets and B-47s. We were not in the least surprised to hear that *Charlie* was the very first private plane, large or small, to land at Sidi Slimane.

From Rabat our next destination was Dakar in Senegal. We would have to skirt the edge of the Sahara Desert on our route where it is washed by the waters of the Atlantic. In this region, for a thousand miles or more, no roads existed, settlements were rare, and airstrips rarer still. We made our preparations with great care. A planned quick stop at Agadir turned into more than two days of waiting because of warnings of sandstorms ahead.

A wind shifting from tail to nose cost us speed and we had to look for a place to land for more fuel. In a pinch ten gallons of ordinary automobile gasoline would work. We put down on the sand at Cabo Yubi and we promptly bogged down. This was the Spanish Sahara and a jeep full of Spanish soldiers came careening down the strip. We tried many words, gasoline, petrol, and after they smiled and nodded that they understood we were in luck because they rolled out a drum of aviation gas.

The next stop was Villa Cisneros [Dakhla], which we expected to be larger, but we again had to stop for gasoline as Dakar was another seven hundred miles away. A gasoline aviation truck pulled up before the propeller stopped and we obtained twenty-five gallons of fuel. Then we were directed to a little inn, hoping for a bed and some food. Amazed, a barefoot Berber in blue gown and turban asked us in perfect English what we wanted. He had learned to speak English from the

British and Americans during the war in French West Africa.

Tay asked him where his home was and he said, "The desert." She got our flying map and asked if he could point to any settlement or any village and he said, "Just the desert."

In the air again and headed toward Dakar we were hungry and dined on the Berber's gift of crackers, Gruyère cheese, and water. Tay was taking a tepid swig when the engine stumbled. For one horrible second we imagined ourselves being forced to land on the beach seven thousand feet below, until I switched the gas selector to "Left." The right tank had run dry. Although we had a gas gauge indicator we were flying by the clock, estimating how much time we had before switching gas tanks depending on the conditions. We were startled—any time the engine stumbles you are startled—we were probably too busy staring down at the shoreline. We calculated that unless we had strong head-winds we would make Dakar with twenty-five minutes of gas to spare.

At that time Senegal was French West Africa. Dakar was the most important city on the Atlantic coast of the continent between Casablanca and Cape Town. We spent ten days in Dakar, so enthusiastically devouring the first-class French cuisine that I feared we would add more weight problems for *Charlie*. This was our Easter vacation and we lingered because we knew for the next five thousand miles luxuries would be nonexistent and even modest comforts rare. Tay solved the weight problem by shipping our winter clothes home.

We swam in the lukewarm ocean waters and fished from a twenty-foot dugout canoe. We were never in danger of sinking, but water was forever spilling over the low sides and there was a need for bailing. We caught king mackerel and a local fish called capitan, some weighing more than twenty pounds.

TAY: Before we went fishing we were watching the fishermen while we were sitting on mounds of sands nearby. While we were watching them we felt we were being watched. It seemed as if one or two men in blue uniforms were popping up and down behind these little sand hills. Finally, they came up to us and said in French, "Monsieur, Madame, come with us." Apparently they felt we were up to something and they took us to the police station. We went in and talked to them and persuaded them that we were just tourists. There were very few tourists throughout most of Africa and they just weren't used to seeing a young, foreign couple watching the locals. And a lot of these people had not seen a little plane like the Cessna.

LOWELL: We really enjoyed Dakar. It turned out that *Charlie* needed some R and R in Dakar too. On a local test ride the plane became covered in oil. When a Pan American mechanic looked over the Cessna we discovered that an oil gasket had disintegrated. Since few small planes flew in and out of Dakar no spare part was on the premises. We had to radio to New York for a new oil gasket. We thought we might be stuck an additional week, but we had the part within a week because of our Pan Am connections.

The day before our departure a Frenchwoman also flying a small plane along the same route to Dakar had run out of gasoline and cracked up her plane. She suffered a broken leg. We were headed to Goundam, located fifty miles west of Timbuktu on the edge of the Sahara. We followed first the railroad and then the Niger River for guidance with a stop in Kayes, a place that boasted of being the hottest in French Africa. When we landed it was 120 degrees Fahrenheit. The Frenchmen doing the fueling were courteous enough to arrive bearing ice-cold bottles of lemonade.

Two hours more flying and we paused overnight at Bamako, which was just as hot, and we spent a breathless night in a one-window hotel room taking turns every couple of hours under the shower.

Goundam was made up of hundreds of mud huts belonging to the natives, a mosque, and a French fort. Tay and I were put up at the fort in what was a *Beau Geste* type of building where the commandant lived. It was fortresslike and flew the French tricolor.

While given the use of a large bedroom we were advised to sleep on the terrace roof because the nights would be cooler. However, during our stay that did not happen. It was humid and rarely did the

Lowell and Tay with nomads in the desert.

thermometer dip below 115 degrees. It even rained a few drops and we rarely saw the sun.

Our host was Monsieur Henard and we followed him on his tours of inspection and got to know the doings of the community, which at the time was becoming a center of trade. Houses had courtyards and one might find a donkey, horse, sheep, chickens, ducks, and children, all of them running about naked. Women hovered over charcoal fires making stews in black pots. Forges were located near the river and men fashioned knives, spears, and daggers. Camel saddles were made nearby. Goods were sold in a marketplace and among the foodstuffs were peanuts, melons, and dried fish. We came upon a butcher shop, but the meat hanging by cords was almost hidden by unbelievable swarms of flies.

A Tuareg chieftain had recently arrived on camelback. He heard about our Polaroid camera which produced a picture in sixty seconds, which we found to be a great way to make friends quickly. This was a fortunate break for us because the Tuareg nomads had lived in the Guandam area for many years unlike the black Berbers of Central

Africa. Tuaregs live in black, goatskin tents and wander on the desert sands. Both groups are Muslims. We quickly seized the opportunity to meet with this chieftain, who was dressed in white robes. Shoes off, I sat on a blanket beside him and sipped sickeningly sweet tea. An odd Asian music played on a string instrument and the chief asked if we cared to see some Tuareg war dances.

What astonished them most was when we played back the songs on our tape recorder and passing out the Polaroid pictures produced almost equal awe and excitement. The chief presented a beautiful leather pillow to Tay and his handsome dagger to me, a royal gift, indeed, one that was really a museum piece. As we left we were asked to return the following winter to share the hospitality of their desert encampment.

Our stay in Goundam ended with the arrival of one of the few black members to the National Assembly in Paris from French West Africa, who was greeted with great fanfare. That night there was a major celebration with drummers and dancers as the center of attention. Crowds surrounded the group of white-robed dignitaries. The deputy's arrival was an important event.

That ended our visit in Goundam and our next destination was the Belgian Congo, although we made a slight detour for a flyover of Timbuktu, a centuries old meeting place of camel and canoe where Tay and I had visited a year earlier when traveling for Cinerama. We stopped for gas at Gao, about 250 miles along, planning just to stay for a short while with the Congo still 1,500 miles distant. A report of thunderstorms ahead, however, grounded us overnight.

The next day we flew two more hours, or another 250 miles, to Niamey, which is part of Niger, and we were headed for Kano, in Nigeria, another 500 miles along for our day's work when all hell suddenly broke loose in the plane. There was a terrifying clatter and a heavy vibration up front. My first thought was that a bearing, or something equally important, had let go in the engine. I was sure we were headed for our first forced landing. Still, the engine kept running, though the clatter and vibration were terrifying. We were lucky because if we had

The Tuareg people in Timbuktu.

kept going the whole cowling could have blown off. Fortunately, our small tool kit carried screws.

We decided to spend several days in Kano before moving on. To our relief we reached the Kano airstrip and we then learned that the noise had been caused by the loss of several screws that were supposed to hold the engine cowling in place.

The day after we reached Stanleyville [Kisangani] there were a series of boat races between the river people and villagers as part of a commemoration of the fiftieth anniversary of the death of Sir Henry M. Stanley, the African explorer for whom the community was named. We were amazed in Stanleyville that many of the local citizens owned Fords and Chevrolets, and by others who owned bicycles. Belgian administrators were everywhere and we even played nine holes of golf with the governor of the province. We had heard that so-called "darkest Africa" was largely a thing of the past, but we were surprised to learn the direction life had taken.

Flying what we considered to be somewhat of a risky route with few places to put down in an emergency, Tay and I advanced to

Paulis [Isiro], a remote village where we were told upon landing on a grass strip that we were the first Americans to ever set down there. As *Charlie's* tail wheel rolled onto the hangar's dirt floor, the ground gave way and the wheel dropped into a termite hole. It took six of us to pull it out again and set it back on firmer ground.

The people of Paulis were in a holiday spirit. Tribesmen we had been told about had come to town to stage one of their remarkable dances. Men and women wore feathered headdresses and loincloths of bark or animal skins as they danced in a great circle, shuffling in the dust, tossing their red-plumed heads from side to side and jingling the little bells on their wrists and toes.

We kept seeing things that we wanted to take home for souvenirs, but every time we thought of buying something we thought about *Charlie* and how the backseat was crammed full like a station wagon and how every ounce counted. We kept saying, "One suitcase apiece." Periodically, we shipped clothing home to my parents and they shipped clothing for the next season onward to us.

TAY: That was always upsetting when I wanted to buy some kind of large souvenir. Lowell would say, "If they're earrings, you can buy them." There really weren't that many souvenirs that we saw at first, but we found a lot more items in the Middle East later.

Before leaving Stanleyville we had made inquiries about trying to arrange a visit to the Pygmies of the Ituri Forest and that was where we headed from Paulis, on our way to seek out Anne Putnam and the Pygmies, a visit that proved to be spectacular and memorable.

13

The Congo, the Rwenzori Mountains, and Kenya

The little surprises that Lowell and Tay Thomas took note of when their airplane with the human name tried to talk to them by making mechanical sounds always disturbed their equilibrium the way high winds created air turbulence. They always created worry and had to be addressed.

While seeking to be thoroughly prepared and vigilant in taking good care of *Charlie*, Lowell Thomas was quick to react when he saw something like oil splashing over the windshield and heard funny noises emanating from the engine. Thomas reacted prudently to those alerts and the minor malfunctions never did anything worse than throw flexible plans off a little.

Certainly as they embarked on their journey, relatives expressed concerns about their health and well-being and some of that concern was directed to how the Cessna 180 would hold up. Thomas may have been a good pilot, but everyone knew that circumstances beyond his control could affect mechanical aspects of the airplane or that unexpected weather conditions could initiate problems. He knew he was going to run into unusual circumstances flying places he had never visited and landing at airstrips he had not seen.

Lowell's decisions, with Tay's observations taken into account, were very much in synch with the moods of the plane. They knew it was their lifeline and they treated it accordingly, very conscientious about making sure it was in fine running order. Still, if you are going to fly ten thousand miles or more, it is difficult to rely on everything running perfectly smoothly every second of the way.

But Africa was one of the most rustic places for small plane flying and that was part of the lure of the trip. For Lowell and Tay, their time in Africa represented a major highlight of the journey.

Planning way ahead, making contact with local officials, and having the State Department documentation in hand supporting their trip also enabled the Thomases to make arrangements to receive mail from home along the way, to post letters, to ship film back to the United States, and to pick up shipments of film to supplement their stock.

As skilled a pilot as Thomas was before departing on the duo's flight to adventure, the daily flights, handling the plane in a variety of environments, helped make him an even better pilot while on this journey and for the years to come.

❖ ❖ ❖

LOWELL: We came out of the jungle, sadly leaving the Pygmies behind, but while still in the Congo we set out to fly to the Rwenzori Mountains, which Tay very much wanted to see. The Rwenzori Mountains were on our "must see" list from the beginning.

After going about seventy miles we saw ahead of us a solid wall of afternoon thunderstorms that stretched as far as we could see to the east and the west. Morning is the time to fly in the Belgian Congo, for convection later builds up the great anvil-topped thunderheads that so often march like cruel giants through the afternoon skies above the almost endless forests. So around we wheeled, beating a retreat. We took off at a much earlier hour the following day.

When we reached Bukavu we had some mail waiting, but our new supply of film was not due to arrive until the Sabena plane landed in two days. This gave us an unexpected layover. We thought we might obtain the governor's secretary's permission to land in Parc National Albert [Virunga National Park], but we were turned down. That led us to fly much farther to the town of Rutshuru where we were told we could rent a car to drive to the foot of Rwenzori.

TAY: The source of the Nile. That was exciting. The Rwenzori Mountains are in Central Africa and they have snow on them most of the year. The mountains are on the border between the Congo and Uganda and the tallest mountain is almost seventeen thousand feet in height. Here I was now flying around it. I couldn't believe it.

People are surprised when they hear there are mountains in Africa with snow on them because they think of it as a hot place. The tallest peaks in the Rwenzoris are among the limited number of perpetually snow-covered mountains in Equatorial Africa. Mount Kilimanjaro, of course, is the tallest mountain in Africa at 19,340 feet. When the native peoples talked about those mountains they talked about "mountains of salt." They didn't know what snow was and somehow that wasn't a hint to explorers either.

LOWELL: The Rwenzoris are also called "the Mountains of the Moon." It's a very significant mountain range. It was interesting that so many explorers didn't know about it or couldn't find it. *Charlie's* roar stampeded herds of buffalo, but had no effect on lazy hippos that clogged the river like logs. Groups of elephants flapped their ears in annoyance and then resumed their peaceful feeding as we passed.

When we reached Rutshuru we were dismayed to learn that no one had a car to be rented. But some British tourists told us that we could cross into Uganda, where there was a small airstrip, and rent a car there near Queen Elizabeth Park. We gained approval for this idea, found the little grass airstrip, and were able to land. We had to buzz off a herd of buffalo grazing at one end before we could set down.

TAY: Africans came running out of their huts and waved to us.

LOWELL: There were no signs of any park wardens or cars, and naturally, no telephone. Where we landed was a little bit of a distance from the chalet and we needed a ride. There was no radio there, so I couldn't raise anyone. We knew that Mweya Lodge was built only fifteen miles away in honor of Queen Elizabeth who had come to open the park only a few months before. We decided to bomb the lodge with a note.

TAY: We flew over to the lodge and I wrote out a note that read, "We are two Americans, coming from the Congo, and will land at Kasengi [Kasenga] where we'd like to leave our plane for a week while visiting your lodge and Mutwanga. Could you send an auto for us? If so, please wave your arms as a signal. Thank you." We put it into a cardboard carton, along with a few stones for ballast, and flying over the lodge at about one hundred feet, I threw it out the window. We were lucky. It landed right down by their flag post. I remember it was a good shot. An African promptly retrieved it and by the time we made our fourth circle, a European man in a bathrobe appeared and waved a towel at us.

LOWELL: Back to the Kasengi grass strip we flew and an hour or so later a young British driver in a Land Rover appeared—the towel waver. It so happened that the lodge was mainly used by British tourists who made reservations well in advance. The accommodations were quite nice, bungalows that included a bedroom or two, a living room, and a porch offering magnificent views. From our bungalow the first evening we could see any number of hippos and seven elephants in a grassy meadow hardly a half mile away. We spent two days at the lodge and made friends with a German woman who gave us a ride around one day when we saw such wildlife as elephants, wildebeest, impala, waterbuck, and hippos.

When we were ready to depart for Mutwanga she offered us a lift. However, when we reached the chalet known as the Mutwanga Inn, we faced some perplexed looks from the innkeeper. Much to our alarm, it was believed that we had crashed in the forest and such a garbled report had gone out. There was quite a comprehensive search for us and our downed plane that included Sabena Airlines and the Belgian military while we had been at the lodge in Uganda, safe and secure, and our plane anchored safely as well.

Where we stayed was at the foot of the Rwenzori Mountains, at about four thousand feet of altitude, and our room faced Mount Rwenzori. For five days we were the only lodgers at the inn and we mostly relaxed and caught up with our correspondence and diaries.

A few other guests arrived and one was a Belgian visitor intrigued by the peak nearest us and with the help of the innkeeper we organized a two-man expedition that included porters and supplies. The Duke of Abruzzi, born in Madrid to the king and queen of Spain, made the first ascent of 18,008-foot Mount St. Elias on the Alaska-Yukon border in 1897, but he was also the first to achieve success climbing the highest peaks in the Rwenzori Mountains in 1906.

TAY: Lowell left me at this nice little camp at the foot of the mountains. It looked like a small motel. It was sort of one story and then it had little cabins and we had a little cabin. It was right on a stream and it also had a little swimming pool, which I used every day. Lowell took off for two or three days.

LOWELL: This fellow and I climbed the mountain in front of us until we hit the snow line. We passed through tall, thick elephant grass, and through a strange forest of banana plants, trees with pinkish bark, and enormous tree ferns. Lunch was at the Kalonge bungalow and as we settled down at a fireplace I dug out of my rucksack the paper Tay had written at Smith College for an African geography class on "The Mountains of the Moon," the mountains we were then visiting. We spent the night in that bungalow.

Higher up, bamboo gave way to gnarled and moss-hung trees that closely resembled cedars, while the ground was carpeted with thick, springy mats of moss that varied in color from green to yellow and even orange.

All afternoon it rained. We headed for a second bungalow that day, but the last hour on the trail was a nightmare, extremely steep and slippery. On the third day we headed up to another bungalow at 14,300 feet. The way was very steep. The slope was covered by vegetation and under foot was a confused tangle of roots. Much of the time we had to scramble from root to root, heaving ourselves from one to the next. Between the roots was a black, watery ooze, into which our shoes disappeared each time we slipped.

That night, fully dressed, even with a heavy sweater on, was by far the most uncomfortable. It was hard to believe that we were only thirty miles from the equator and it was so cold. The next day we reached the fifteen-thousand-foot level and it was tempting looking to the top, but special permission was required to set foot on the summit of any of the Rwenzori peaks and we had not had time to obtain it. By then we both also had headaches brought on by the altitude and the exertion. Luckily, we started down in sunshine.

I rejoined Tay at the camp and we borrowed somebody's car—it wasn't as if there were rental companies right there—and drove through Queen Elizabeth Park.

TAY: We were in the middle of all the wild animals. There were hippos in the water and there were elephants all around. We could hear them up close and we passed an elephant where the car was not even up to the top of its legs. The car was a very small thing and this huge elephant was up on a hill above us. It decided to charge us, waving its trunk. We just pulled away gradually, and then we looked back to see him waving his trunk, perhaps in frustration.

LOWELL: That was before the car broke down. It just quit. It had a vapor lock, I think, or water in the gasoline. We sat for several hours and then I thought maybe if we could bypass a certain part of the engine, changing the gas flow, I could make it work. I used an enema bag that we had in our gear to drain the carburetor. Tay sat on the hood of the car and held it up in the air and it drained to where it needed to go and we got the car working. American ingenuity.

TAY: This was a very lonely place. We never saw another car. It was a bad place to get stuck. This would have been a good time for AAA to help us out, but there was nobody out there, absolutely nobody, but we made it back to the plane and took off.

LOWELL: Our next stop was Nairobi, in Kenya. Nairobi was pretty much the British headquarters in Africa. There was a strong English presence there. They had the New Stanley Hotel and a lot of scenes in the movie *Out of Africa* were set in Nairobi. Of course, the movie came out much later than our trip.

Kenyan independence from British rule, what they called "Uhuru," did not take place until 1963, but the Mau Mau Rebellion, the first revolt, was underway when we got there. Bad timing in that sense, although we did not feel as if we were in danger. The Mau Mau was an anticolonial group and starting in 1952 they led an uprising. Much of the focus was on the local white landowners, trying to drive them out of the country and force them to give up their lands. For the first several years the violence was on the outskirts of the city in isolated pockets. But while we were in Kenya, the British military was responding. They ran bombing campaigns on the rebellious groups.

TAY: The environment in the city was fairly civilized, but Lowell was asked if he wanted go to flying with the British bombers. Can you imagine going on a bombing run like that? We weren't going to bomb anybody, but Lowell did go and I stayed back in the New Stanley Hotel and felt very sorry for myself—it was my birthday.

LOWELL: I flew along with the bombers and took pictures of what they were doing. They were trying to quell the rebellion and bring peace back to the country. At the time the British portrayed what they were doing as more or less a police action and we didn't really know what was going on in the country. It took about a decade to completely sort itself out, but by the end of that decade and that revolt, the British were no longer in Kenya and Kenya was an independent nation. We were there for the beginnings of that without knowing what would come in the future.

I think we were in Nairobi for four or five days, but when we left the first thing we did was to fly to Mount Kilimanjaro. They call Kilimanjaro "the Roof of Africa" because it is the highest mountain on the continent at more than nineteen thousand feet. Seeing it for the first time is so spectacular: the snow-covered cone of the summit, standing alone and high against the background of the land. In the plane we were able to climb high, but not to the summit area.

We got up to seventeen thousand feet. That was about as high as we could go because of the altitude and thin air. We didn't have oxygen with us and the plane itself was not made to go any higher. Tay said she really felt the thin air. So did *Charlie*, I believe. We had to circle and circle to get as high as we did with the weight we were carrying.

I had seen the Himalayas and walked over mountain passes there on the way to Tibet, but the perspective was completely different. In the Himalayas I was on foot and in that mountain range there are so many mountains close together that are very high. Kilimanjaro is by itself. To see one great mountain standing alone, that was really quite a sight.

If you have been in Colorado, most of the mountains are about fourteen thousand feet high, all about the same, so no one mountain stands out. Even near Anchorage with the Chugach Range, all of those mountains are around five thousand feet, The Himalayas are like that with many of those immense mountains about twenty-six thousand feet. Kilimanjaro is not surrounded by any other similar-sized mountains. In that way it resembles Mount McKinley in Alaska, which also stands out alone against the landscape, with no other mountains anywhere nearly as big around it.

After circling Kilimanjaro, which is actually just beyond the border in Tanzania, we landed the plane near the mountain. The name *Tanzania* was not applied until 1964 and before that the land was known as Tanganyika for a while. But showing how volatile that region and area was, Tanzania had previously been the British part of German

East Africa until after World War I. Also within Tanzania, one of the zones of governmental supervision is Zanzibar.

We spent the night on the slopes of Kilimanjaro in a small cabin owned by an Indian man whose job was running a sawmill on the lower slopes of the mountain.

TAY: It was just a cabin with two bare bunks for our sleeping bags, but no outhouse. I remember very well there were elephants around it at night. I did not want to go outside to the bathroom, even to flush a toilet, in the middle of the night. There also could have been a lion there. If we saw lions we wanted to see them from a safe distance.

LOWELL: It was upward and onward from there. We flew northeast to Somalia, right along the coast of the Arabian Sea. It is bordered on the other side by Ethiopia. The main way we have heard about Somalia in the news in recent years is about the acts of piracy of the people who raid boats and take refuge there. It's along the water, right on the coastline, but the interior is mostly made up of desert. We landed at an airstrip and there was a Shell Oil man there. He helped us get situated for the night.

TAY: He was the gasoline man for ships that stopped in. It was hot there. We had to sleep in his library on cots and I remember it was still one hundred degrees at night. When we were in those African countries it was midsummer and it was really hot everywhere in the national parks and elsewhere. It must have been 110 degrees most of the time. If we went up higher in altitude at night it wasn't nearly as bad, but we couldn't do that every night.

LOWELL: We were traveling in an Africa that no longer exists today, that was beginning to go through transition after World War II when the colonial era was coming to an end. The British, the French, the Belgians, and Germans had at one time pretty much divided up Africa to their liking. The Germans lost most of their influence after World War I.

Now the peoples of Africa, in several of these countries, were at various stages of demanding independence. It would all come to pass, sometimes with a lot of bloodshed, sometimes without any, by the sixties.

We were tourists in Africa at an intriguing time. Our trip was taken before the nations threw off their connections to the European nations and before their own leaders took over to create independent countries. What we saw in many places was the vestiges of an old way of doing things that in the years to come might not be around. We were fascinated by everything.

In some places we saw camels. Once, we saw a lion cub that Tay thought was so cute, as if it was a house cat. It was milk fed. In many of these countries, women were second-class citizens and they covered up wearing burkas. Tay said she thought she would be better accepted if she wore a dress rather than pants and she also pointed out in how many places it was one hundred degrees.

TAY: I visited with some of the women along the Niger River wearing sarong-type dresses wrapped around them. They were doing their dishes there and I thought it was the dirtiest water I had ever seen. At one point we noticed some men carrying urns of water. It was for our showers. They were prisoners and that was their work detail. I don't think very many of the people we encountered in small villages had ever seen a white person except for the French provincial soldiers, or if they were near the airstrip the local man on the scene who handled gasoline for Shell or any oil company.

LOWELL: Thinking back on all of the places we went and how we sometimes tried new foods and had to get by on what we could obtain, you couldn't make a trip like that and be a fussy eater. That would make it very difficult. If you had dietary restrictions of any type that would make it a challenge. You had to be adaptable and eat what you could get, when you could get it. And you would want to have some anti-dysentery pills with you, for sure. We drank tea and it was probably from rainwater, not from a river.

Watusi warriors performing a tribal dance near Nairobi.

After we left the Rwenzori Mountains area we went on to Astrida [Butare]. No plane had reached the community in a few years, so when we showed up some two hundred people turned out to see us. Astrida reminded us of a small, midwestern US town with several stores, a gas station, and many stucco homes. We stayed in a comfortable hotel, but we were awakened late one night with loud rumblings and a severe shaking of the whole room. We were in the middle of an earthquake. We were unaware that area of the Congo was prone to earthquakes.

We managed to rent a Ford and drive twenty miles to Nyanza, the capital of the Watusi [Tutsi] people. A large number of spectacular dances were assembled for our pictures. The Watusi were immensely tall, handsome and striking in short, brightly colored skirts of red, white, and blue. They carried spears or bows and arrows and wore anklets of bells and leopard-teeth necklaces, and most spectacularly they wore headdresses of flowing white plumes.

Africa is a continent of many countries and they differ greatly in custom, wildlife, geography, and peoples. While there are similarities between the environments of some neighboring nations, there are huge differences between those with jungles and forest and those with deserts, just as the climate differs rather markedly between Alaska and Florida in the United States.

As we left behind the tallest mountains in Africa, we were putting Kenya and the Congo, the Pygmies and the Watusi, in our rearview mirror and the next stop for Tay and me was Ethiopia.

14

Following the Nile to Cairo and Wadi Rum

Although it was the rainy season when Lowell and Tay set course for Ethiopia they knew that for the next period of time they could expect tremendous heat in the places they hoped to visit. So many years later Lowell still remembers the heat well, with temperatures soaring over 110 degrees Fahrenheit regularly and even touching 120 degrees.

It is said that Alaska is an Arctic desert, but that's because of its dryness, not the temperature. There was a romance attached to the sands of the desert, however. Lowell Thomas Sr. had helped make his reputation as a war correspondent by following Lawrence of Arabia in his desert campaign during World War I.

The Middle East was joined at the hip with biblical times, as well. Legends and lore, religious stories passed on throughout history, all were linked to the sands. Moses wandered in the desert for forty years. Persia was the forerunner of Iran. Ancient Babylonia was a predecessor of Iraq. These places were all talked about in religious schools, in Sunday schools.

These desert places represented the cradle of civilization, the birth of religions, the sands of time through their sands. For Lowell and Tay, the lure was powerful to see Jerusalem, to visit the places ingrained in their minds since their youth. Even the image of sand dunes sometimes blowing particles in the wind, the hills of sand that one had to crest to see over, were like magnets for the Thomases. Tay wanted to hold a fistful of sand in her hands and let the grains fall through her fingers.

Ethiopia had also been very much in the news in the twentieth century. Before the outbreak of World War II it represented a country of African independence to American blacks, free from colonialism. There was huge attention paid and great mourning when Italian dictator Benito Mussolini proclaimed Ethiopia part of his empire in 1936.

The British Empire and British Commonwealth nations, joined by Ethiopian irregulars, fought back in 1940 and 1941 to wrest Ethiopia from Italy during the East Africa campaign. The Italians surrendered after the Battle of Gondar in November of 1941.

Ethiopia is regarded as one of the oldest strongholds of mankind, dating for certain to the second millennium BC. It is considered the origin of *Homo sapiens* perhaps dating back four hundred thousand years. Ethiopia was referred to in the *Iliad* and the *Odyssey*, in the Old Testament in Hebrew, and was called Abyssinia.

The most important figure in twentieth-century Ethiopia was Haile Selassie I, who in 1916 began the work of modernizing his country, and in 1930 became emperor. He was called "the King of Kings" and his reign far outlasted the time period when Lowell and Tay visited. He was deposed by a Soviet-led coup in 1974 and died in 1975. Although the capital of Addis Ababa is the principal city, it was not so anointed until 1886. However, scientists believe that mankind spread from Addis Ababa beginning about a hundred thousand years ago.

❖ ❖ ❖

LOWELL: When Tay and I left Nairobi, Kenya, we were bound for Addis Ababa. The distance was more than seven hundred miles and most of the country in between was mountainous and without roads.

Another choice was to fly roundabout through Italian Somaliland, which would be oppressively hot. It was also noted that there might be hostile tribesmen along this route.

By choosing a third alternative we could stop to refuel in Mandera, a tiny British outpost where Kenya touches Ethiopia and Italian Somaliland, and spend the night in British Somaliland, and we set out to follow this plan. It was a long time before we saw any settlement, but we circled Wajir three times as a prearranged signal, and although our map indicated one road to follow from Wajir to Mandera beneath us we saw four roads leaving the village. We employed some trial and error before we picked up the Dawa River and followed it to Mandera.

The moment we landed, hundreds of Africans came running from all directions. Two British soldiers, the local administrators and the only Europeans at the field, came running up too. They had no word of our coming, they told us, and were surprised by our arrival. This came as a shock to us because if we had been forced down no one would have known about it and no attempt would have been made to help us. The British were concerned about the breakdown of their communication system and we were even more so.

Our next leg was to Hargeisa, the capital of British Somaliland, some four hundred miles ahead across a land with no roads, no radio, no nothing. We had to reach Hargeisa before dark and we had to make the flight by compass. As we approached we saw ominous clouds ahead, but we just slipped under them.

Next morning we departed for Addis Ababa and landed at the big, up-to-date airfield. However, officials blew their tops when we told them we did not have a flight permit—the local American Embassy had it. Just as we had premonitions of being led off to jail, two embassy men arrived and cleared up the situation.

Addis Ababa was a city of surprising contrasts. Palatial homes sometimes had huts for next-door neighbors. Many streets were modern and well-paved, but with donkeys and carts making up most of the traffic. A large outdoor market cluttered with cattle, sheep, and goats was near a modern department store.

TAY: When we got to Addis Ababa we were at eight thousand feet of altitude and it was nice and cool at night. We shared a bottle of wine and, combined with the lack of sleep in the lowlands and the altitude, the room was whirling around.

LOWELL: Due to fortunate timing we were invited to a ball in honor of the birthday of Emperor of Ethiopia Haile Selassie I, although he had not returned from a trip to the United States. The embassy procured a tuxedo for me and a white halter dress for Tay and we were the guests of Ambassador and Mrs. Simonson and their daughter. At the dinner many of the dishes were unidentifiable to us and we sampled them conservatively although there were many different kinds of bread and meat pastries. The whole affair was formal and we found it difficult to converse effectively with anyone.

We did have a meeting with the crown prince and he seemed very interested in our travels.

TAY: We were told to bow upon greeting the prince, but we were taken right in to him and shook hands because we thought we were being introduced to a lower level functionary. They were very high on formality, but no one seemed to begrudge us our mistake. To make up for it we bowed dramatically on our way out.

LOWELL: Most people that we encountered expressed interest in our journey and they were always very interested in *Charlie* and how we traveled so far in such a small plane. Again, there was virtually no tourism in these faraway places at the time so they did not meet people like us dropping in very often. At that time there weren't very many people just traveling for the adventure of it.

Several times in Africa we marveled at the heat. It was wonderful to see another part of the world and to see how different it could be in the desert, Saudi Arabia, and places like that, but I wouldn't want to live there. At some places it was 120 degrees and it was the hottest in the countries of the Middle East. But it was so dry that if you could get into the shade it was more bearable.

I suppose we reacted to the sands and sand dunes the way some people do when they visit Alaska and see miles and miles of snow-covered land stretched out before them. The most vivid image of the desert for me was the red sand "mountains." I associate them with Arabia, but with new borders of countries and the like they are part of Namibia today. There is a clay and salt pan surrounded by reddish dunes. The colors are spectacular.

TAY: We flew on down the Nile—the Blue Nile originates at Lake Tana in Ethiopia. The White Nile branch runs from Lake Victoria. We passed a lot of waterfalls. We left Addis Ababa for Asmara, the capital of Eritrea. As we flew along the Nile we passed large collections of ruins. We flew very low over the water and there were these huge ruins from earlier days and it was quite a sight.

LOWELL: We were running behind our flight plan, though, overdue to Asmara, and yet running low on fuel in search of Assab, a small port on the Red Sea. We couldn't find it. The map showed far too few details of the Danakil Desert and I noted the land below us was growing rougher. There were no roads to follow and no towns. I tried to set an accurate compass course and we had about an hour's worth of fuel left. Eventually, we spotted what seemed to be an abandoned airport. We taxied up to the biggest hangar and saw battered signs in Italian, but there were airport attendants. We were able to send a wire to Asmara and it turned out they were worried about us.

In Asmara, Tay and I learned there were American troops there operating a radio relay station. The greatest attraction of all was the chocolate milkshakes available—we each had two.

The next day our flight had us crossing two hundred miles of the Nubian Desert, flying mile after mile over sand dunes and sandy levels where nothing but an occasional rocky hill broke an otherwise featureless desert. There was no detail we could follow as we made our way to Wadi Halfa on the Egyptian border. From there we headed to Cairo, where Tay and I had previously visited and seen the pyramids

Making a tape recording of what he sees in Cairo in 1953, Lowell Jr. at age twenty-nine.

and the Sphinx. We were arriving in July when the heat, the city's flies and smells were at their worst. We had no desire to linger in the city.

We had now left Africa behind us and were in the Middle East. The only reason we paused in Cairo on our way to the holy city of Jerusalem was to check in with the Egyptian Civil Aviation. If we had not, we ran the risk of being shot down by the Arabs on one hand or the Jews on the other. Israel was very much a new state and there remained high tensions in the area—as there still are. Because of this the route we were required to take was not the fastest. Since we had come from Cairo we had to stay over Arab lands so we were required to swing wide over Jordan. Instead of flying the two hundred miles straight to Jerusalem we had to fly over a much greater distance—and we ended up landing at a new airport in Jordan about one minute from the border.

There was a no-man's land between Jordan and Israel and it was heavily fortified. I was able to film, but was warned to make it snappy because I might be shot at as another correspondent already had been. We stayed with Arab soldiers and that was troublesome for Tay.

TAY: Certain problems arose because I was a woman in the middle of a Muslim Army camp. I found it necessary to wear the one dress I had with me that had sleeves and a high neck. I tried to be as inconspicuous as possible, but I felt all eyes were on me. One time I know that was true. I was standing by the roadside waiting for Lowell and a company of recruits was marching by. Just as they reached me the sergeant barked an "Eyes right" command in Arabic and instantly I had the whole company staring directly at me as they marched past.

LOWELL: Another day [we were] filming with Jordanian troops. We filmed a Sten gun operator without ammunition. When he worked the bolt action, the gun fired imbedding a bullet in the sand about a yard from Tay. She said she had enough of being at the front lines.

TAY: Visiting Jerusalem was a bit like going back in time. It had been the crossroads of the religious world forever. I bought some very beautiful, painted wooden pieces that were scenes of early Christianity. They were pretty much miniatures or otherwise I would not have been able to carry them on the plane—no room. These were tiny and I still have them. Our passport stamp is what required us to land in Jordan. But we had a wonderful stay in Jerusalem because we knew a family that went back to Lowell's father's day. They founded an American colony in Jerusalem.

We went to their little house there and went swimming in the Jordan River. We tried to go swimming in the Dead Sea, but we couldn't. You could only lie on the top and float because of the salt content. It is almost nine times saltier than the ocean. It was so buoyant and so salty it was sort of awful. We didn't stay in the water very long. You couldn't sink. I gather it is even worse now because it's all drying out, evaporating. They've also dammed various places on the river tributaries so that's reduced the flow into the lake. People just have to destroy everything.

LOWELL: After that we went to Petra and Wadi Rum in southern Jordan, which are right near one another. Petra was written about in a poem, something about being "a red rose city half as old as time." There were fantastic ruins there. The city dated to about 300 BC. Wadi Rum was Lawrence's headquarters during the World War I desert campaign. We weren't trying to retrace any of Lawrence's trails, but we had heard about this place and Petra's ruins and there was a fort with Jordanian soldiers nearby.

They came out with camels and we rode the camels into the fort. We had a young Jordanian man with us at the time as our interpreter and he wasn't a bit happy about the landing. He didn't like flying. They took us on the camels into this red stone fort going through a little crack. It was like the Old West in books by Louis L'Amour. You get through the crack and it opens up and you see the city behind the wall. It was very beautiful. It was pretty rough riding the camel. That was a first for us. You jog up and down. It's not like riding a horse.

TAY: When we left Jordan we headed to Beirut and at that time it was called "the Paris of the Middle East." We stayed at the most beautiful hotel, right on the water. The Mediterranean Sea was a clear blue. When I say right on the water, the hotel was on a pier reaching out into the water. You could eat dinner on the pier. I remember eating a whole avocado. I'd never had a whole avocado before. It was such a beautiful city and I feel sick about what happened to it with the war. There were wonderful shops, a French influence. It's all changed. So sad.

LOWELL: We made our longest open water crossing of the entire trip—about a hundred miles—to Cyprus. That was probably Tay's least favorite flight because she doesn't like to lose sight of land. The engine sounds rougher when you go above ten thousand feet and it makes it worrisome for her. You realize the engine could quit and there isn't any place to land. Flying over water is a gamble in a single-engine plane.

Then on September 12 we flew to Ankara, Turkey, and then went on to Istanbul. I spent a week seeking permission to climb Mount Ararat

Tay visiting with King Abudullah of Jordan.

although there was skepticism over whether Noah's Ark ever came to rest on the 16,946-foot mountain, despite the belief engendered by the book of Genesis. Tay, suffering from an ear infection, needed rest. The authorities would not grant permission for me to climb the mountain. Then we were thrown out of our hotel because of a convention—the only hotel.

While Tay was ill and put on penicillin, we were taken in by the Pan American station manager. I learned that Cinerama was going to make its Middle Eastern debut in Damascus as part of an international fair. I flew there without Tay to observe the new process's reception, but a fellow named Bill Kayser, who was a Pan Am mechanic there with some time off, volunteered to fly with me.

Amazingly, one day the Syrian Army had to be called out to maintain order at the theater for the showing of *This Is Cinerama* in Arabic. That was our introductory show to Cinerama with scenes from around the United States. Shipping film to New York from Istanbul was a difficult process, so we detoured to Beirut, and that gave us a late departure when we left Damascus to return.

From Damascus to Istanbul was more than seven hundred miles and I ended up flying in darkness, losing all visual landmarks, and without being able to reach anyone on the radio, as the gas supply ran down. Eventually, I reached the tower, but there was cloud cover and I couldn't see the city. I broke out in a cold sweat. In fifteen hundred hours of military and civilian flying I had had my share of nervous moments, but none of them had ever equaled this. All I had to count on was belief in the instruments.

We were atop a solid cloud layer, but I was counting on a forecast of improving weather. I held a constant heading, dead reckoning, unaware of a change in wind direction. Ankara was the only alternate landing sight, but Bill and I decided to continue. After more than five hours in the air I knew *Charlie* was nearly out of fuel, so I called the tower and asked for immediate clearance. We got it.

Charlie broke out of the overcast at two thousand feet with the runway lights to port. I rolled *Charlie* onto the final approach, and then with flaps down, I set up a slight power approach. I was congratulating myself on our good fortune when "cough, splutter." We were out of gas and the engine had quit. The plane was still at five hundred feet and it was sinking too rapidly to make the end of the runway. I flipped the gas tank selector to "both" in hopes there were a few drops unused. The engine caught and surged for perhaps two seconds, then pulled for another two seconds. That had been enough. We barely cleared the runway, the wheels touched, and we bounced before settling down. I told Bill he would have a story to tell. It was bad judgment on my part stretching the fuel.

To reach the terminal and parking area we had to call for the gas truck. The tanks were completely dry after flying five hours and twenty minutes. Once again, God was my copilot. That was one of the closest of close calls I ever had flying. You always remember those, you certainly do.

TAY: I was on the ground and I just knew that something was going on. It was bad weather outside my window.

LOWELL: A little later Tay was feeling better and we left for Iran, flying into Tehran, where I had once landed as a passenger in a jetliner.

Soon after arrival we had an audience with the Shah and Queen of Iran, who were agreeable to posing for pictures. I had met Mohammad Reza Shah Pahlavi on my first trip to Iran and I knew he was an aviation enthusiast. He seemed quite impressed by *Charlie's* performance. Everywhere we traveled, if we had time and were staying long enough, we attempted to go through channels to make arrangements for taking photos of the Shah, or the king, or the emperor. It was a different time and it was a little bit easier to drop in on royalty, I guess. I'd say more American tourists were exploring Route 66 by automobile with their families than were going overseas.

Tay and I ended up visiting the Caspian Sea for a story on how Iranian caviar was the best, not the Russian caviar. Although politeness demanded that we taste endless samples, neither Tay nor I are too fond of the prized dish. By the end of the day we felt like sturgeon ourselves.

TAY: You see very little caviar in your travels in the United States unless you look for it and we saw barrels of it. They would just dig in with a sort of wedged knife and give you great big hunks of it on your plate. I did not like it much at that time, but wouldn't you know I developed a taste for it later. I'm ready to go back.

LOWELL: I'd rather eat Alaska salmon.

Then we had trouble clearing customs and getting out of Iran. It was because of all of the stuff in the back of the plane, the cameras and such. They made us take it all apart and looked at everything and it took about two hours in the heat. When we finally got away, heading for Meshed [Mashhad] at the border with Afghanistan, we didn't think of Tehran as a place we could turn back to in case of bad weather.

15

With the Nomads
in Afghanistan

Making friends with the Tuareg chieftain some months earlier had planted the idea strongly in Lowell and Tay's thoughts that they would like to spend time with nomads. They had been invited to spend time with this man's nomadic group and it was something they very much wished to do—as long as they could find it wandering in the desert. That did not pan out, but through perseverance they ended up visiting with another tribe of nomads.

The modern view of Afghanistan is that it is an extremely troubled place, teeming with hatred for Westerners and, with little interruption since 1979, a nation that has been torn by war and different masters. For nearly ten years between 1979 and 1989, the Soviet Union was bogged down in a fruitless campaign that some have called Russia's Vietnam. It was a hopeless war that left Afghanistan in tatters. Then, after the bombing of the World Trade Center Twin Towers, the attack on the Pentagon, and the hijacked plane that crashed in a field in Pennsylvania on September 11, 2001, Afghanistan became a focal point of a fresh war. The United States, still occupying the country with troops in 2013, sought to oust the Taliban fanatics who had taken over the ancient country.

However, despite this recent sad history, Afghanistan served as a beacon in the ancient world. The Silk Road, the old trade route, passed through Afghanistan. It was part of the Persian Empire. There are suggestions that humans have lived in Afghanistan for fifty thousand years. Alexander the Great and his Macedonian army at one time, though only briefly, occupied Afghanistan.

Fascinated by peoples of different cultures and customs, Lowell and Tay were intrigued by Afghanistan's ancient history and wished to spend time with natives of the country experiencing their way of life, a way of life ingrained for centuries.

After living with the nomads, soon after the Thomases were dining with royalty and national leaders of other countries. What they didn't know was that their trip of a lifetime was going to end soon, a little bit ahead of time and for a reason they did not anticipate.

❖ ❖ ❖

LOWELL: When we arrived in Meshed in northeastern Iran, known as a place of martyrdom, the American consulate gave a reception in our honor. While we were grateful for the hospitality, we were more focused on jumping off to Afghanistan, which had long been a forbidden country for visitors, than in local sightseeing.

Our permission to land in Kabul had necessitated months of correspondence between the American Embassy and Afghan officials. We were warned we would not even be able to obtain airline gasoline. However, almost miraculously we stumbled across an American in Beirut who ran a seasonal airline for pilgrimages to Mecca and said we were welcome to some of his gasoline in Kandahar. He was the only one who could have solved our problem. We were put up at the Morrison Knudsen construction camp, the American firm building dams in the region, and that was a treat because of the supply of American beer and ice cream. We did some filming there.

On the last stretch into Kabul we passed over what we took to be a column of soldiers in the desert, but after coming closer at a height of five hundred feet we realized it was a group of nomadic people, most of whom waved, though one of whom threw a rock at us. American

Embassy staff greeted us with relief that we hadn't gone missing en route and His Excellency Abdul Wahab Tarzi was especially interested in us. He recalled my father's visit thirty-four years earlier in a Buick touring car that he managed to get over the Khyber Pass in what might have been the first automobile in Kabul.

Although Kabul was a growing and modernizing city, Tay and I were most interested in finding a way to travel with a band of nomads. Most of the rest of Afghanistan was still undeveloped and very backward and it's a very rugged country. A little bit to our surprise, Afghan officials liked this idea. We were granted permission to travel to Khost, which was ordinarily closed to foreigners, and supplied with a translator.

The governor of Khost, Abdul Rahman, frowned on our plan to rent horses and ride out in the desert until we found a band of tribesmen willing to take us along. Instead, Abdul Rahman insisted that he help us find a "trustworthy" band. Soon enough we were traveling thirty miles by jeep with Amin, our interpreter, into the desert to meet up with such a group.

The eldest tribesman, whose name was Safy, shook hands with us. He was bearded and in his seventies and he invited us into his tent. He wore a dusty white turban and a faded, ankle-length robe. We came to the point slowly, as one must in the East. I explained that we had heard much of the tribes of Afghanistan and that we admired their determined struggles for independence. We hoped that we might pass some days with his band so that we might tell the people of America how they lived.

Without a moment's hesitation our elderly host said that Allah had surely guided our footsteps and that he and his people would be happy to have us, whether for a day, a month, or a year. Whatever was theirs was ours. Allah and they would be our protectors.

We joined these people who were migrating to the Indus River Valley, going right over the border into Pakistan with their animals. We immediately rolled out our tent and erected it. Tay caused a bit of sensation by using a primus stove to cook soup.

Lowell hanging out with some tribesmen in the desert.

It seemed we were part of two clans traveling together. They had come more than halfway to their winter pasture on the frontier with their flocks of sheep and goats and more than a hundred camels. This fall migration took a month since the animals stopped to graze. Safy, and Gulbehar, the other leader, said that their young people never gave up the nomadic way of life to flee to the city, but that above all they wished they could have their own land for permanent settlements. Departure time the next morning would be at 5:00 A.M. The plan was to cover twelve miles and get to their destination by afternoon so the animals could graze. By the time we were ready, others had been on the trail for an hour. When we had difficulty loading our gear on borrowed pack animals a couple of nomad experts laughed at us and had it packed in no time.

The people and animals that preceded us churned the trail into deep dust. Our shoes sank almost out of sight. We plodded on mile after mile. Where we were, everything was dust, but farther away

Fulfilling one of their aspirations, the Thomases accompanied some nomads in the Afghan desert as they broke camp and made their way to Pakistan for the winter.

were green slopes and pine-covered mountains. Far to the north the snowy summits of the Hindu Kush stood against the sky. As we passed through settled areas, women and little girls fanned out on either side into the already harvested fields for anything that might burn in that evening's campfires.

As we walked they drank water that had been obtained from irrigation ditches out of goatskin bags. This was a lifestyle that had been in place for centuries. It was not like anything we had seen in the United States in the middle of the twentieth century.

The elderly and weakest people rode on the animals. There was also a little puppy and I remember chickens getting the free rides. Sometimes we were given eggs to eat. That was a sacrifice on their part to give us food.

Tay reached a point of collapse and a tiny donkey was thrust under her. It was so small that Tay's feet dragged in the sand until her

Tay's infamous donkey ride with the nomads in 1955.

new friends among the women caught her as she threatened to fall off. Eventually, they tied Tay's legs to the donkey with dirty rags.

TAY: When I had enough I climbed off the poor donkey and went back to Lowell and the other men. For lunch we had peanut butter, Afghan bread, and tea. Then I boiled pots of water to refill our canteens. The women again stared at the stove. "How I must puzzle them by cooking just plain water," I thought.

The women did most of the work, unloading the camels and putting up the tents. The tents were made of animal skins. I think they were black wool. They were not manufactured tents. It may have been wool from their sheep. The older girls were the ones that collected pieces of bark that may have fallen off trees in their aprons to save for later for the fires at night. They collected dung too. It was a very basic level of existence. The women did wear beautiful jewelry. It was made of turquoise and it looked like maybe even little diamonds. We were told that was the wealth of the tribe, invested in that jewelry, and, of

An Afghan woman in the desert.

course, camels. That was another way to measure the wealth of the tribe. The women wore necklaces and bracelets and wore woolen skirts and tops. Everything else went on the back of the camel. It was like us with the back of the plane.

LOWELL: After dinner of boiled potatoes and tomatoes that were gifts from the governor of Khost, supplemented by cans of corned beef hash and fruit, we talked with visitors, but were falling asleep from our hard day by six thirty. Chief Safy offered to delay the start the next day since we weren't used to the tribe's early rising time, but we felt it best to fall in with their regular schedule. We asked to be awakened at four thirty, but we were awakened by complaining camels and braying donkeys and were shocked to find that it was five thirty. Apparently our friends had thought it impolite to waken us. The encampment was already packed.

That day's walk was only two hours so we readily caught up. It seemed to us that these people lived on a near starvation diet, their meals consisting mainly of bread, curds, and occasionally rice. We thought the bread was delicious. But we wondered where these people found enough energy for the hard lives they led. It troubled us to see children scrape out our empty food cans, and they actually fought over our leftovers, melon rind, bits of tomato, and moldy bread. After a few days with them we were within a half hour's hike of Khost and I satisfied myself that *Charlie* could land safely there. I asked Chief Safy to take good care of Tay and he took my request seriously.

TAY: I went into the tent for a little privacy and the chief posted a guard just outside. He brought along a gun and a water jug and his authoritative yells kept everyone at a distance. He even threw stones at chickens that came too close. I think I might have rather walked back with Lowell, but the guard sat in front of the tent the whole time and he was wearing one of those bandoliers with the bullets. He was very authoritative and the gun was very obvious. I tell everybody that Lowell left me alone in the middle of Afghanistan.

LOWELL: I was back over the camp in an hour and a half, but everyone was so excited that it was difficult to clear them off the strip.

TAY: It was actually very scary because they had never seen a plane and they all wanted to run toward it. I kept saying, "No! Back up! Back up!"

LOWELL: I recall cutting the engine very quickly and stopping the prop as fast as possible because I saw these people running toward the airplane and I thought someone would get hurt. I let Safy and Gulbehar sit in the plane. Most others were content merely to look at their first airplane, but a few could not resist touching the shiny metal, though they did so gently, almost reverently, as though *Charlie* was the most fragile thing in the world.

After dinner I turned on the plane's radio, picking up programs from Kabul, Karachi, and New Delhi and bringing in beautiful symphonic music from Moscow. The men had a dance for us, going around

One of the Afghan tribal leaders, Safy (center).

and around in a circle and hopping around. Their music seemed a little odd to us as they sang. They were fascinated by the plane and the radio. They were all sitting in a circle around the plane.

In the morning the camp made ready even earlier than usual. Hundreds of other nomads were going to flood into this area and this tribe wanted to reach its destination in order to stake out its place with good water. Chief Safy and some of the other men who had horses stayed behind to see us off.

We circled over the tribe and turned to the west. The few days we had spent with that band of Pashtun nomads had opened our eyes. For generations these people had been described as quarrelsome, unfriendly, and distrustful, but we had not found them so. A few days before we had come to them as strangers, but when we left we were friends.

As the nomads walked on, we flew on, also to Pakistan, to the city of Karachi. If given our choice we would have skipped Karachi, but we had to stop there for political reasons to explain ourselves and seek permission to visit areas of the country that were normally off-limits.

Part of our pre-trip planning involved contacting anyone who might have influence or connections in the places we were headed. In New York, Laurie Shaffi, the Pakistan Consul General, was very helpful, but we had no idea how involved he would get in making us feel welcome in his country. When Tay and I landed, basically right from the Afghan desert, we were dirty and disheveled, wearing blue jeans and other beat-up clothing. We were shocked to be met by a limousine sent by the prime minister. We had a very short time to spruce up and then we were whisked to lunch with Prime Minister Muhammad Ali Bogra, who had previously been ambassador to the United States and had a genuine fondness for our country. At one point I interviewed and filmed the prime minister on his miniature golf course while he was trying out a putter given to him by President Dwight D. Eisenhower.

From Karachi Tay and I were granted permission to fly the Cessna to the Karakoram Mountains region. We were bound for the Hunza Valley in an area where Pakistan, India, and Chinese Turkestan come together. We made a brief stop in Rawalpindi to pick up Tay's sister, Frances Pryor, who was joining us for a last fling before getting married. A little shopping was necessary to buy boots because we were in sneakers and it was going to be cold and snowy in the mountains.

We were the first ones to be granted permission to fly to this area, but when we stopped for refueling at the military field of Chaklala they didn't know about it and sought to prevent us from going on. Wire transmissions to Karachi, however, clarified matters. The return message from Karachi read, "They're mad, but let them go."

We lessened *Charlie's* load for the next leg where he had views of Nanga Parbat and perhaps a glimpse of K2, the second tallest mountain in the world. The Hunza Valley had been on my mind since visiting Tibet in 1949. It was another place that I considered to be "out of this world." The landing gave us the creeps because a nine-thousand-foot-mountain wall seemed only a few yards away. I was thinking Frances may have been ruing her decision ever to board the jet in New York.

After the hairy landing we were bound for Chalt, about thirty miles away by jeep on a road that was gravel and sand winding through boulders, and to Hunza, which is located at about 8,200 feet of altitude. Near the Hunza River the trail was barely wide enough for the jeep, zig-ging and zagging upward at an incredibly steep angle, traversing shear walls that rose above it into obscurity.

TAY: This was northern Pakistan and, gosh, the jeep ride was unbeliev-able. The road was so rough and so narrow. I was sitting on the outside and I could look down and it was hundreds of feet to the river below. At Chalt it got too rough even for the jeep and the next day we got horses, little ponies, which Lowell said were like the ones he saw in Tibet. There were lots of times when the trail was so narrow that the horses walked on the very edge of the trail because they were used to having packs on their backs that hit the side of the rocks. We were on foot at that point. There was one bridge across a river and it was a rope bridge. It had wooden pieces for steps and some of them were missing. You had to step over them. I think we did seventeen miles one day and twenty the next. We spent the night in a little stone hut along the road. It had a little, tiny fireplace, and it was very cold, even in sleeping bags.

That night I was lying on the stone floor in that hut and I felt so tired. In the middle of the night, all of a sudden, I thought, "My gosh, I think I'm pregnant." We had been married for five years and I had wanted to get pregnant, but we never did. Out of the blue it hit me. And I was.

LOWELL: The morning after our arrival on the Hunza side of the val-ley, Tay woke me with a nudge to the ribs and when I opened my eyes she gave me the startling news that she was going to have a baby. She had to repeat the statement before its meaning really sank in for it was the last thing I expected to hear. I would have been dumbfounded even if back home, for after nearly five years of wanting children and having none, I had given up thinking I would ever become a father.

I was thrilled, but alarmed at the position that confronted her. We were in one of the most remote regions in all the world. We were in the world's most rugged corner. It took two agonizing days to con-tact the Pakistani doctor in Gilgit over a primitive, battery-operated

Tay and Lowell examining a map while in Bahrain.

telephone. One had to shout in order to make the phone whisper at the other end. Our instructions were for Tay to rest until she felt strong enough to ride out on horseback, but only to do so in slow stages.

TAY: I felt ready for anything. We had a crystal clear day for our departure. The snow-covered giants, white plumes trailing from their peaks, encircled us. I was aware of every jolt, thought it was the bumpiest ride I'd ever had on a horse, and that it would never end. But the trip from Chalt to Karachi seemed a swift dream compared to those days on the Hunza Trail.

LOWELL: We flew from Karachi to Bahrain where close friends Max and Leila Thornburg lived on their own island off the coast and where we spent Christmas of 1954. Max had been in Bahrain for Standard Oil since the 1930s. We swam in the pool and in the Persian Gulf, fished, spent hours by the fire in the library, and sailed the waters about the island in the Thornburg dhow.

An Arabian dhow in the Persian Gulf, one of the sights from the Thomases' yearlong flight to adventure.

As Tay continued the visit with the Thornburgs I decided to hitch a ride on a larger freighter dhow for a week to see what life with the descendants of Sinbad would be like. I found passage on the *Faras*, which is Arabic for horse. It was sailing for the Pirate Coast of Oman and although no one else spoke English, by using a translator I was able to convince them to take me the 360 miles through Qatar. The captain led morning prayers in Arabic each day; I was the only infidel aboard.

There was a fight between an Omani and a Bedouin at one point. I conversed with a Bedouin man through an interpreter, with difficulty, and learned about his life. After we had been out a couple of days the captain collected the fare of ten rupees from each passenger. When the ship's trip ended I flew back to Bahrain. There Tay and I began formulating plans for our return home.

Before making our way home we wanted to have Tay checked out by an American doctor if we could. Using his connections Max arranged for us to enter Saudi Arabia to stop at the Aramco Oil operation where there were seven thousand American employees. What we did not know was that a request for us to fly *Charlie* into Saudi Arabia required the approval of King Saud himself.

Tay was checked out by the American doctor who had delivered many a baby and while he said that she was fine, he recommended that we not stray much from the beaten path and stay as close as possible to medical attention. Then we sent a note to the king's attention asking to be received. Ordinarily one would no more expect to be received by His Majesty than by the rulers of the Kremlin in Stalin's time, but my father had been received not long before. Tay and I were invited to come to Riyadh. However, Tay suffered an attack of the grippe and I flew to Riyadh alone.

I was met by Sheik Abdullah, the king's secretary, and he beckoned me into a royal limousine. In the speeding car, with me wondering what the rush was, Abdullah said, "His Majesty has invited you to dine with him. We'll just make it."

Dinner was orange juice, soup, mutton, potatoes, spinach, a lettuce and tomato salad, boiled chicken, rice with almonds, and Jell-O, oranges, bananas, and apples for dessert, served by waiters in spotless, white, Western-style uniforms. When the king rose, everyone instantly got to his feet. The meal was over, whether any of those others present finished eating or not. We made our way to a huge parlor. I was invited to sit just to the left of the grandest chair of all. Coffee was served at once.

I was granted the opportunity to photograph and shoot film of the king in his garden the next day and he invited me to another meal, allowing me to shoot and film while he was eating. When I closed in for a final shot, His Majesty spoke his first and only English to me. "Just one more?" he said.

Back at Aramco I was invited to take a ride in a single-engine jet to the Empty Quarter which had first been explored in the 1930s and 1940s—my map was still marked "unexplored." These mountains of sand forever reflect the force of their maker, the wind. Graceful, rippled, delicate ridges and an infinite number of symmetrical patterns mark them.

Once reunited with Tay we made plans to head home. She was

Lowell, his trusty plane, and local tribesmen in the Arabian Peninsula.

a little envious of my experience in the Empty Quarter so I suggested an alternative route to Cairo. With the prospect of spending the night in Ubaila, an Aramco desert station, we became the first to traverse the Empty Quarter in a small plane. When we arrived we took a swim in a pool at one of the few houses and it was pointed out to us that the water had "the largest beach on earth."

We were back in Cairo, where we had thought to sell the Cessna, but we did not. We mostly retraced our steps to Paris, our last landing of the journey on March 4, 1955, a year after our departure from Toussus-le-Noble Airport. There we had the plane dissembled and *Charlie* was shipped back to the United States. We flew back to New York and there waited for *Charlie's* return as cargo.

Back in the United States, we worked on a book about this once-in-a-lifetime adventure, and on August 10, 1955, our first child, our daughter Anne, was born.

16

North to Alaska

Flying throughout Europe and Africa on their own, with their own plane, was an adventure for young people and one that could not be easily duplicated. Lowell and Tay Thomas estimated that they flew fifty thousand miles on the journey from Paris to Paris with more than a few stops in between. Lowell certainly gained small plane flying experience that would serve him well for the rest of his life. He tackled trying circumstances and variable weather conditions. He learned how to get out of tight spots and adapt to changing conditions.

Once their great journey was completed, the Thomases settled down back in the eastern United States. Tay gave birth to their first child and they were no longer a youthful married couple with an itch to travel and no responsibilities. They still retained their youthful spirit, their spirit of adventure, and their desire to see the world's most exotic places, but they balanced it with home life and the realities of being parents.

In the mid-1950s, after Lowell and Tay returned to the United States, Lowell resumed working for his father's productions, which by then included the television series *High Adventure*. It was an hour-long TV program and Lowell Sr. asked his son if he could help out

Lowell with baby daughter, Anne, who was born in late 1955.

with some projects. In 1957, film projects led Lowell Jr. to Alaska for the first time since his 1940 mountain climb with Bradford and Barbara Washburn.

Alaska struck him as a fantastic and beautiful place, not coincidentally a place that offered adventure and might also be a good place to raise a family.

LOWELL: Only a few months after returning from our trip around the world, Tay and baby Anne, riding in a laundry basket, and our German Shepherd dog named Boaz, were all flying together in the Cessna 180 to Jupiter, Florida, from New Jersey to visit Tay's parents for Christmas. That December 1955 flight was one of the closest calls I ever had flying in my million miles in the air and it was the only forced landing I had with my entire family aboard.

We were flying over the Atlantic Ocean coastal swamps of Georgia about twenty miles south of Savannah at about seven thousand feet with a planned next stop in Stuart, Florida. With no warning the engine began to shake violently, lose power, and backfire. It felt as though a wrench had been thrown into the engine. This was nothing that could be corrected in flight. Obviously the engine was failing. I turned around quickly. The lights of Savannah were still in sight, thank the Lord.

TAY: It was very quiet in the plane except for the engine. I didn't panic, but I said to Lowell, "Oh, quick, turn it off, it sounds awful." He said, "I think that's the best thing to do," and he did it.

LOWELL: I asked Tay to use her flashlight to look at the map and find the closest airport. It turned out to be Hunter Army Airfield, a Strategic Air Command base, located a bit northwest of the city. In all my miles in a small plane I had not experienced this type of shaking in the engine. It was a first. Our staggering engine hadn't completely quit, but we were giving up a little bit of altitude every second. I asked Tay to give me Hunter's tower frequency. We put out a "Pan, Pan" call [an emergency call]. The military tower came on the air and asked what the problem was. I explained and asked for permission to land. "Approved. How many souls are on board?"

Our sick engine gave us enough power to reach the base with its twelve-thousand-foot-long runway. I pulled back the mixture, shutting down the engine for a dead-stick landing. As we rolled along the runway, two jeeps with armed men pulled up on either side of us. We got out. Boaz jumped next and waited while I attached a leash to his collar. Then Tay reached back and gathered up Anne, still sound asleep. They kept us in a waiting area while they checked us out to see if we were legitimate.

TAY: Finally, I said, "Look, I've got to feed my baby. Can you get me some milk?" They brought us some milk and filled the bottle. The dog was wonderful. He just sat beside us and took it all in. The baby was fine too, but she was hungry by then.

LOWELL: They could easily see that we were legitimate and once they opened the engine they could see we definitely had a problem. We were given a lift in one of the jeeps to operations while the airmen pushed the plane to a tie-down location.

At operations the officer of the day heard our story and then located a nearby motel and had us delivered there. Next morning, back at the base, we opened the engine cowling and soon found the problem. We had a damaged cylinder. Later, a mechanic discovered that a valve had broken and fell into the cylinder, in turn breaking the piston.

Why were we greeted with those armed men in the jeeps? General Curtis LeMay was checking security measures at all SAC [Strategic Air Command] bases. As a test he had recently sent a C-47 with a dozen men into another base unannounced and those men scattered around the base undetected. For all the Hunter officers knew we might have been put up to our surprise landing. But when they saw our engine they knew we weren't faking it.

We ended up taking the train to Florida for the holiday, leaving the plane at Hunter until a new engine could be sent from Wichita, Cessna's home. Tay and I were glad the engine failure hadn't happened ten months earlier while crossing the Mediterranean at the end of our yearlong journey. It was frightening to have something like that happen with your family aboard, but the engine held together long enough for us to escape a truly serious problem.

In 1957 my dad decided to do a show on the DEW (Distant Early Warning) Line in Alaska and Canada, the radar system constructed to guard against Soviet planes invading and bombing us during the cold war, and the role that the Air Force was playing in protecting us.

Dad and I came to Alaska (while Tay stayed at home expecting our second child) with a film crew and I was the advance man to set things up. We had a large film crew and the Air Force provided transportation, a C-54 and a C-47 to get the crew around. I think we flew

In the late 1950s Lowell helped make a film about the nation's cold-war defense systems in the Arctic and some of the DEW line radar is behind him.

into Ladd Field in Fairbanks to start. From there we took off for the far north along the DEW line to see what they were doing. We were near Barrow along the coast of the Arctic Ocean. The filming included the scrambling of fighters. It put in front of an American audience what would happen and what we could do if the Russians started to invade.

While I was in Alaska I was caught up in all of the publicity of how they were trying to obtain statehood and I started thinking that well, we've got a new state coming along. President Eisenhower signed the Alaska Statehood Act in July of 1958 and I was thinking we ought to do something more about Alaska than just talk about the Air Force. My father thought that made sense too, and we followed up.

In 1958, I flew the Cessna 180 to Alaska with Tay and Anne, who was two and a half. David was only twenty-two months old, so we left him with two sets of adoring grandparents for a time. Noel Wien was a pioneer Alaska bush pilot who made the first flight between Anchorage and Fairbanks in 1924 and then started his own small airline. He made that flight in an open cockpit plane, a Hisso Standard J1.

That summer Merrill Wien, Noel's son, and I, both flew Cessna 180s around as we filmed, both of us carrying the camera people. Alaska made a very powerful impression. It impressed me that this was where I would like to live. I started to think that way on the 1957 trip and when Tay came in 1958 she caught that same spirit too. We loved the wilderness, the outdoors, the wildlife, the great expanse. It was sort of the old idea of "Go West, young man." This was going west to the frontier. That really appealed to me.

Back in 1940 Alaska had made a good impression on me with that mountain climb, but I was only sixteen at the time. I had not finished high school and I was not in any position to move to Alaska. I was in a different place in my life. I saw enough of Alaska to think, "Gee, what a wonderful place." There were terrific mountains and glaciers and no crowds, all that wilderness. Great place to live. So that really solidified it, that 1958 trip, and Tay agreed with me that it would be a wonderful place to move, to our new state, to the frontier. It was put in our heads that was what we were going to do, although it took a couple of years to make it all work, till we could really make the move in 1960.

It was also very obvious to me that Alaska would be a great place to be a pilot and have an airplane. After that 1958 trip we were especially glad that we still had *Charlie*. We flew it back to Princeton, New Jersey. We kept using it down there as we had before to make local trips round-trip until we made the move north.

I had gotten to know Herb Hilscher. He was the most prominent public relations man in Anchorage. He kind of helped set things up for us when we were moving to Alaska and that gave us a head start, like where to look for a house and how we could get settled in. Our first year we rented a house that was in the Turnagain area of Anchorage. The owner was moving someplace else. We stayed there for a year and then we decided we wanted to have our own place. We found a newly built home, a split-level with three small bedrooms, still in the Turnagain area overlooking the water that leads to Cook Inlet. By that time we had a growing family too. Our son David was born in 1957, so the kids were not born in Alaska, but they were very young and they grew up in Alaska. Anne was about five by then.

There seemed to be every indication when we came to Alaska that I would be able to continue flying regularly. That was a great enticement and opportunity and that would not be true just anywhere we chose to live in the United States. Aviation played such a big role in my life it's hard to picture it not being part of me. I always enjoyed it. I'm not even sure how to explain it. There's a lot of freedom when you're flying. You're on your own and you can look down at the rest of the country. That was great. To me there was just something special about that, which was super. I never wanted to give up flying as long as I lived, but I finally did when I turned eighty-six.

One reason that we moved to Alaska was the sense of newness about the new state. But for Tay and me it also meant getting a new start in a new place on our own. I was very close to my father and everybody in the country knew him because of his radio and TV. There were some advantages for me. I made that trip when I was fifteen with the Navy and I went on that mountain climbing trip with the Washburns when I was sixteen. Those were through my father's connections. He was so well-known that it gave me entrée to some places that would otherwise have been difficult to visit. Tibet, of course. I think it was a very fine asset, no question about it and we had a very fine relationship.

My dad was frequently full of good ideas for me of things that I should do and so forth and sometimes that got to be a little bit too much. Coming to Alaska we removed ourselves from being so close to Tay's parents and to my parents, all of whom were famous in their own ways. Coming to a new state was somewhat symbolic. It was getting a new start, getting away from the old, traditional things and striking out on our own. When I told my parents that we were moving to Alaska, my dad, who had been there, said, "Boy, that's a good move. Good thinking."

TAY: My father didn't blink an eye because he was a vice president with Pan American and they flew around the world so Alaska was just

While Lowell flew more than a million miles before he retired, wife Tay flew her share with him, on their yearlong flight to adventure trip in 1954 and 1955 and before and after that journey.

a hop, skip, and a jump for him. I loved Alaska from the first time I saw it and we were not just in Anchorage. We spent some time in Fairbanks and some summers in Talkeetna. We flew around Mount McKinley and we landed on glaciers. I remember taking Anne for a walk every day down to a park while Lowell and the others were busy filming on Mendenhall Glacier.

One time we were hanging out with the camera crew and there was a place that kept baby animals. They wanted to get a picture of Anne feeding the little baby moose. They put her in the pen with the moose and I held my breath. She was holding her bottle of milk out to the baby moose. I don't think the moose understood what was going on and it turned around and started to kick. The camera man dropped the camera, rushed in, grabbed her, and carried her out. Anne was fine. It hadn't scared her, but it scared me. Anne handled the whole trip very well. That's her personality, even today.

But I fell in love with Alaska. I just fell in love with the whole state. Frankly, we were a little bit anxious to get away from our families. It just felt like the right thing to do, to get away from the hubbub in the east. Lowell's father wanted us to live in Princeton in a boardinghouse and I wouldn't have anything to do with it. I told him so. We made quite a bit of money doing the lecture tours and we were able to buy a cute little house in a small subdivision of families our age. We made a lot of friends there. That was one of the happiest periods of our early married life.

We had our own house, but it seemed as if we had to go to Pawling or Greenwich every other weekend. My family wasn't so bad because my parents were busy with my five younger siblings. But Lowell didn't have any brothers or sisters so he was very much in demand. So I really welcomed the change and I know he did too. Alaska was much more civilized than I thought it would be.

Some of my family and eastern friends didn't understand much about Alaska and they were very worried that we would be so far away and with their grandchildren too. Both my parents and Lowell's family came to visit almost right at the beginning. They saw the little house we were living in and the area that looked like a treeless, bare suburb, as it had been built recently. We did decorate with about twenty of the flags of the countries we had visited.

LOWELL: When we moved from Princeton on May 24, 1960, I flew to Akron, Ohio, to Madison, Wisconsin, to Grand Forks, North Dakota, to Winnipeg, Manitoba, to Dauphin, Saskatchewan, to Edmonton, Alberta, to Fort St. John, British Columbia, to Watson Lake, to Pine Lake, to Juneau, Alaska, Yakutat, and to Anchorage on June 1. Then I returned east to drive the family up in our old International Travelall. I replaced the backseat with a big mattress so the two kids and the dog could play or sleep for the two months we were on the road.

I actually think our family in the east was envious in a way. We had found a new frontier. In a way what we were doing was a traditional thing in the sense of American history and going west and moving away from our families. Some of our friends in Princeton thought we were crazy.

TAY: The Princeton gang did not understand. When our friends gave us a farewell party I remember two of them gave us Aladdin oil lamps because they didn't think we were going to have electricity in Alaska.

LOWELL: We differed from the Washburns. They had lives in both places, Boston and Alaska. They would come to Alaska in the summer, go on an expedition, and then go back east and live the life of any easterner there. When we moved, we moved. There is still a mystique about Alaska, but it was even more so then. Fewer people had visited the state and there was a lot of publicity about it as a new state emphasizing the indigenous peoples, their igloos in winter, dog teams, cabins, and fantastic mountain scenery.

TAY: When we rented that house in Turnagain it was the first new subdivision in Alaska. The funny thing was that after everybody worried so much about how cold it would be and stormy, we had no snow at Christmas that first year. The kids were running around in shoes, not boots, playing outside. Anchorage is milder than most people think. They think the temperature is always below zero in all parts of the state and that it's dark all winter.

LOWELL: Alaska very much so had a history of airplanes and small plane flying, and flying is still important to the state. That was a big attraction for me. Alaska was really opened up by the airplane. Even today Alaska is more dependent on airplanes than any other state. Through history Alaska has the mail delivered to remove villages by airplanes. Bush pilots fly people to a number of villages where there are no roads. I grew to appreciate that history too, as I learned it.

When we moved to Alaska it was my goal to keep doing what I had been doing: writing, filming, telling stories, and flying. I did some projects for the University of Alaska in the beginning. I did a project for Wakefield Fisheries too, down in the Kodiak area. It was an advertising film. It kept me busy and brought in some income.

The University of Alaska asked me to do a promotional film for them that had a great deal to do with Arctic research and ice islands. I teamed up with Bill Bacon, who was in the 16-millimeter business, my specialty. I was doing the same type of thing that I had done in the Lower 48 for my father's television show. At the same time, right from the start, I began developing another illustrated lecture about Alaska that I could take to the lower states in the winter, the off-season. I kept that going for a number of years. I was good at it and I enjoyed it. I went from an illustrated lecture about Tibet to an illustrated lecture about the trip Tay and I took around the world to a lecture about Alaska.

17

Earthquake

O n March 27, 1964, the second largest earthquake in world history, and the largest in North American history, struck Alaska. The epicenter was roughly eighty miles from Anchorage in Prince William Sound and one of the hardest hit areas of Alaska's largest city was the Turnagain neighborhood where Lowell Thomas and his family lived.

The earthquake, which measured 9.2 on the Richter scale, was violent in its intensity and shocking in its five-and-a-half-minute duration. The massive quake devastated portions of downtown Anchorage and triggered tidal waves that not only caused huge loss of life in Valdez and Chenega Bay, Alaska, but tremendous property damage in such communities as Seward, Whittier, Seldovia, and Kodiak, Alaska.

There was no school that day because it was Good Friday and it was closing in on the dinner hour, anyway, so more children were home than would have been if the quake struck earlier in the day and they were in class. The population of Anchorage and Alaska was much smaller a half century ago, so fewer people were killed, injured, or lost their homes than would have if such a monstrous earthquake occurred in later decades. Still, the effects of the quake were demonstrated by the fact that people were killed in Crescent City, California, from a tsunami generated by the earth's shaking and that was about two thousand miles from Anchorage.

Only one earthquake has ever released more force than the Alaska Earthquake. A few years prior to the Good Friday Earthquake, the South American nation of Chile suffered through a 9.6 quake. That remains the world's biggest earthquake. Numerous other earthquakes have caused more damage and killed more people than the 131 who died from the Good Friday Earthquake, but in sheer magnitude, the Alaska quake remains the second biggest ever.

On that Friday in Anchorage there was still a considerable amount of snow on the ground even though the calendar had technically turned to spring. Temperatures were below the thirty-two-degree freezing mark, but not excessively so.

For the Thomases it was a somewhat routine day. Lowell had business in Fairbanks, so late in the afternoon he climbed into the Cessna 180 to fly himself the 360 miles north to the largest city in Alaska's Interior. Tay was home cooking dinner, minding Anne and David, who were watching television.

Lowell had just left town, but Tay was home in what was about to become the hard-hit Turnagain area. It was also Tay who became one of the main chroniclers of the quake through her report to *National Geographic* magazine that ran in the July 1964 issue.

❖ ❖ ❖

LOWELL: I was in the air when the earthquake hit, heading to Fairbanks. I had gotten involved in politics and I was going to Fairbanks to give a talk at some sort of meeting for the Republican Party. I heard some conversation on the radio between an Alaska Airlines flight on its way to Anchorage and the tower. The pilot was asking if anybody had checked the runway or something like that. I didn't really know what they were talking about at first. It was shortly after 5:30 P.M. I was going to be getting up there just before dark so I was going to be staying there overnight.

TAY: I was home with the kids. I had been very active with the Easter Seals drive for the Alaska Crippled Children's Association and I was tired. I was supposed to go and see a woman and I decided against it. I would stay home with the kids and relax. The weather that day was actually fairly miserable, kind of rainy and cold.

Anne and David and I were relaxing, watching TV on our big bed, and Anne went into her room. She said she had a headache. She was having some eye problems. David was sprawled on the bed watching some kid program. I went to Anne to comfort her. I took my shoes off and she already had hers off. We were all three wearing blue jeans and cotton tops.

The window in Anne's room looked out over the water and faced the area where the Fort Richardson Army base was. Just after five thirty I heard a rumble and I thought it was the guns at Fort Richardson. That's what it sounded like. But then everything started to shake. We had had one earthquake, a very, very mild one, and that time I remember we were sitting at the dining room table and watched the trees waving back and forth. Lowell said, "Oh, look, it's an earthquake. Let's just watch it. Don't worry. Stay put."

This one felt different. I went to Dave and said, "I think we're having an earthquake. Let's go watch it outside." He protested that he was in his bare feet, but Anne came along with me right away and we all met at the top of the stairs. It was a split level house, so it was just three steps. By the time we got to the hallway the house really started to shake and I said, "Come on, let's go." I opened the door and just stepped into the snow. Dave was still saying, "Oh, my feet, it's cold." They were little kids at the time. The shaking was so rough that I couldn't stand. I simply couldn't stand up. I was thrown to the ground and of course the kids were thrown to the ground. We were about ten feet beyond the front of the house. I have no idea to this day where the dog was at this time. I don't recall him going outside with us. This was Boaz. He loved the kids. But I didn't think about him because I was concentrated on the kids. I turned and looked at the house and the first thing I heard was the cracking of the windows. Then the next thing I saw was the foundation beginning to crack.

After I saw the foundation begin to crack the whole front of the house fell in. I was just stunned. At that point the ground began to break up around us. I had been hanging on to Dave from the moment we landed on the ground. I put my arm around him and was hanging on to him. Anne was a little bit further off and I called to her and said, "Quick! Come, let me hold you!" She came over and the three of us lay there. I had my arms around them, each arm around them, and we hung on to this little piece of ground that we ended up on. It was about the size of three-quarters of the dining room table, maybe a few feet by a few feet.

There were pieces of broken up ground all around us, a mixture of dirt underneath and frozen ice on top. We were hanging on to the frozen top and it was all moving. I noticed the ground moving and parts of the house were moving with us. I could feel this motion of going down, moving down, and I thought, "Oh, the whole hillside is collapsing into the water." Which it was.

I yelled, "Hang on! Hang on!" Dave was crying, but Anne was her usual calm self. Nothing ever fazed Anne. From the time she was a child she was that way and at that moment I was glad she was that way. Then a swing, part of the swing set that was in the backyard, floated past us and I thought, "That's odd. It was in the backyard. How can it be there? It was behind us and now it's on this piece of ground going past us." Then the greenhouse passed us. We had a little greenhouse and it was also on the other side of the house. It was just sitting on a big slab of ground and floating by us. There wasn't a pane of glass broken. The whole thing moved. It was very odd, but it just continued and continued that way.

The earthquake was five and a half minutes long, which is an eternity for an earthquake, but it felt like five and a half hours. I thought, "The world must be falling apart." I didn't really associate my situation as being in it. I just thought that everything was happening all around me. I looked up in the sky and I really thought that at that point maybe I would see God and he might help us or something. I looked up and really thought I saw a vision of a group of people in white robes up there. At that moment I felt a tremendous, intense feeling of peace, real peace. I had not been afraid. I guess I'd been too shocked to be afraid. I always acted strongly in the middle of a crisis and after it was all over I would fall apart. I was hanging on to the kids and I felt this wonderful sense of peace. We finally hit bottom, the bottom of the hill, still sliding on this piece of ground, and we stopped right at the edge of the water.

We stopped and I looked behind me. There was this new cliff. It was all dirt and there were broken pipes sticking out of it. One pipe had water dripping out of it. There were wires all over on the ground and they were going, "Pftt, pftt," that crackling sound. I warned the kids, "Be careful. Don't go near that. Those are live wires." Dave began to calm down. Anne wanted to try to get out of there. There was a little spruce tree leaning against part of the cliff and she said, "Can I try to climb that tree?"

On one side of us was water and in back of us was this huge bluff. I told her she could try if she wanted to and she went over, but it was solid ice. It had begun to rain and everything was icing up. I said, "I think we have to walk along the side of the bluff and look for a way up. It's hopeless here. It's too high. You hold on to me." So we held on to each other and began walking through the debris and the snowy ground mixed with dirt. It was very hard going because we had no shoes on. We were barefoot, and of course we were still wearing our shirts and blue jeans. Dave then said, "Oh, it's cold, Mommy. It's cold." And I could hear his teeth chatter. Poor little boy. There was nothing I could do. My feet were numb already.

We passed our neighbors' house, the Meads. They had been right next door to us, but their house had also gone down the cliff. I hadn't even seen it at first because I was so busy watching ours. Theirs had gone out further into the water and I saw two of their little kids, Wanda and Perry Mead—they had five children. The girl was seven years old, a close friend of Anne's. The little boy was a friend of Dave's. Those two were on the hood of the car (later I learned their older brother had brought them out of the house, put them there, and told them to stay there). Then he went back into the house, according to the youngest sister, and picked up the baby and brought her outside. But the boy then disappeared in a crack with the baby and neither was seen again. She also told me that her older sister was at a friend's house. She survived, but always regretted she had not been home to help. Her mother had made a quick trip to the market and also felt guilty. When I passed the two children on the car I had called to them, and this was a hard decision, but I said, "I don't think I can handle four kids your age. Stay on the car. You'll be safe and when I get up on the top of the cliff I'll get someone to come down."

LOWELL: I had heard only that snippet of breaking news about the quake on the plane's radio, but I didn't know what it meant. I then learned that there had been a great disaster in our particular neck of the woods. It was not until I got on the ground that I heard anything more. When I landed I heard more of the same. There had been a big earthquake down to the south and people had heard over shortwave radio that it was a big disaster and a lot of houses had been lost. Nobody knew for sure exactly just how bad it was, but I just knew something awful had happened.

My thoughts turned to getting back home as fast as I could. I had my plane, but it would be faster by jet. I decided to leave the Cessna in Fairbanks after I got word from Merrill Wien that he was going to be making an emergency flight to Anchorage and that there was room for me to go along. I'm not sure what time of day it was when the flight was arranged. It was dark by then.

So I flew back to Anchorage with Merrill, but Anchorage International Airport was out of commission. The tower was down. We flew to Elmendorf Air Force Base. Some kind of emergency headquarters had been set up and Genie Chance, a radio broadcaster, was on the air. She was sending out messages to people for those who couldn't reach one another. She would say, So-and-so should call a member of the family to let them know they were alright.

TAY: It took about thirty minutes more for us to get to the end of the bluff where I hoped it wouldn't be so steep. Once there I wasn't completely sure we could climb it. Then two men appeared at the top and they saw us and called out, "We'll be right back." Anne and Dave began crying because they thought the men had deserted us. But they were spreading the word and sent some other men to collect the two kids on the car. Then these men appeared at the top of the bluff again, this time with ropes and coats. One came down and picked up Anne and wrapped her in a coat and carried her up. The other one came down for Dave and carried him up. A third man helped me get up the bluff. They put us all in a car. It warmed us up. We did have on an odd assortment of jackets, but we were still cold and shivering for a while before we felt better.

Then they asked me, "Where do you want to go?" I said, "I don't know. Our house is gone. I don't want to go to our neighbors near the water." I had begun to worry about a tsunami coming in and so I wanted to get away from there as fast as possible. It was then that I was beginning to feel fear. They said, "Well, we can take you somewhere up on the Hillside if you want to go." I thought of our church and said, "Yes, you can take us up to St. Mary's and we can stay with the minister and his wife." Someone drove us that way and I remember going across the railroad tracks between the subdivision and the main part of town and the lights were flashing and the horns were going. It wasn't that a train was coming, but that the earthquake had set the whole thing off.

We were driven to St. Mary's Church and the minister was not one bit happy to see us. Their home hadn't been damaged at all, and their furniture was still in place, but all the dishes had fallen out of cabinets so the kitchen was a mess. The minister had just taken his wife and young children to stay with another neighbor. He said, "I'll find someone who will take you in." Then he brought us a platter of roast beef remnants. It was ice cold, but delicious. So we chewed on that for a while and another couple came to get us. They lived fairly nearby on the Hillside and their home had no damage at all.

There were a lot of strong aftershocks that night that terrified us and our hosts wanted to go into the bedroom. We said, "No!" We didn't want to leave the couch because it was right next to the front door.

Every time there was an aftershock the three of us ran for the door. It was very scary, but the nice couple that took us in didn't understand. The aftershocks were much scarier to us then that what we had been through. They turned the radio on for us and all of a sudden we heard, "Does anybody know the whereabouts of the Lowell Thomas family?" Much to my surprise the telephone was working, something which was a rarity in town at the time. So I called in to the radio station and told the lady we were staying at so-and-so's house. By this time it was about four-thirty in the morning.

LOWELL: I had not known what happened to my family for about twelve hours and I was very concerned, very worried. I just had no idea. I had heard about the two Mead children being lost in Turnagain and that probably made me more frantic. Everything was questionable, up in the air. I didn't know what was going on at home or where they were.

TAY: After we reached the radio station I watched down the road, a dirt road, one that was very bumpy and covered with ice and mud, and after a while here comes Lowell in our truck and I thought, "My goodness! We still own something after all." The truck had been parked at the airport where he had flown from earlier in the day and it survived the earthquake in one piece.

LOWELL: That day after the sun came up I went to our house to look at the damage. I found Boaz, our dog. He was OK, but he was howling. He knew something terrible had happened. We also had a couple of cats. The mama cat headed for the box of laundry in the basement and the cat had her one kitten with her. Then I went back with Tay to look at the damages. The kids came with us and we had to borrow clothing for them and almost none of it fit.

TAY: We found most of our clothing in the wreckage. Everything in the bedroom section survived. The bedroom section was above the main part of the house and just sort of slid along and didn't fall apart. So we got our clothing, but almost everything else disappeared or was broken by the collapsing walls. That was a turbulent time for everybody, and some people did leave Alaska for good. One of our neighbors left with her young son, a friend of Dave's, and she never came back. The next morning at the church two men from the *National Geographic* magazine showed up. They knew me from the stories Lowell and I wrote on our flight to adventure. They said, "We want you to come back with us to Washington to write your story." I said, "I'm not going to leave my family. I'm not going to leave here, period."

They offered me a deal of writing and handing them in a page a day while they were in Anchorage gathering other material. So Lowell got stuck with the kids and the dog while I wrote. It was probably a very good thing for me to do because it was right after it happened and I just poured everything out. I didn't worry much about being precise with the words and the grammar. The interesting thing was that the *Geographic* told me later that it was one of the few articles they ever printed that they hardly changed a word.

Alaska was home by then. We were fully committed to Alaska. Our families, who had been concerned about us moving here in the first place because of the distance and the cold and snow, were much more worried after the earthquake. In those days, with most communications down, it was a challenge for people to get word out to loved ones around the country that they were OK. Ham radio operators did a good job and I think that's how Lowell's father heard we were alright. But my mother and father were in Hawaii and the first thing that they heard was an alert of a possible tsunami headed their way from an earthquake in Alaska. They had a nervous five or six hours and then Dad got through to Pan Am in Fairbanks and got word from them that we were safe. Those were harrowing times, but after that the only thing to do was to start over with anything we had left.

LOWELL: That was a pretty scary time. Tay had quite a time of it with the kids. Even now if there is an earthquake of any sort she tenses up.

TAY: Even now when I go into a room somewhere, or a restaurant, I always look around to see if there is a good way out. It seems as if it was another life, so long ago, but I have never gotten over anything that reminds me of the shaking. If I feel someone walking across the room and the floor shakes, I get into a panic.

LOWELL: I missed all of the shaking, but I was just thankful that my family was safe.

18

Flying Alaska

Whether it was making films, shooting pictures, writing scripts, developing lectures, or doing work for hire to promote a university, a government agency, or a private organization, Lowell Thomas Jr. discovered that Alaskan projects took him all over the vast state of 586,000 square miles.

Flying a small plane in Alaska proved to be not so different from flying a small plane in the desert countries of the Middle East. The snow substituted for sand, but there were huge distances between communities and many times those communities were small villages.

Thomas's jobs had him flying the friendly skies of Alaska—and sometimes the less-than-friendly skies when the weather turned nasty. He flew tourists sightseeing, delivered people from small communities to the bigger cities, hauled hunters to their camps, and flew for pleasure, just for the freedom of it.

Eventually, despite having the trusty Cessna 180, Thomas expanded and acquired a second airplane that he also possessed and kept at the ready for decades. The Helio Courier was designed in the late 1940s and went into production in 1954. The models were offered for sale between 1954 and 1974. They were lightweight, single-engine planes that could carry thirty-six hundred pounds and had a range of nearly fourteen hundred miles. The plane's projected ceiling was just shy of 21,000 feet, which in Alaska terms meant barely higher than the altitude of 20,320-foot Mount McKinley.

❖ ❖ ❖

LOWELL: Alaska was just made for aviation. Given the elements and how the wind and the weather can change on you, I think you almost have to be a bold pilot to fly in Alaska for a long time. It comes with the territory if you are going to fly in the bush. Maybe if you are a multi-engine plane pilot it's a different story, but flying a single-engine plane it's always tricky. There's always something out there waiting to get you. The elements are more of an issue. There's more risk flying in the bush than there is flying a big jet commercially.

I think I have been most everywhere in Alaska by plane that you can go, but I never kept track of listing the places. Let's see, Barrow on the Arctic coast and Juneau, the capital in Southeast, Fairbanks, Bethel, the Aleutian Islands a little bit, Anchorage of course, Ruby, McGrath, Unalakleet, Shishmaref, Point Hope, Kaktovik, Prudhoe Bay, Sitka, Ketchikan, Yakutat, Skagway, Tok, Delta Junction, North Pole, Gakona, Glennallen, I've been to them all. I think I've been everywhere there was an airstrip of some sort probably. Talkeetna, of course, Dillingham, landing on the glacier at Mount McKinley, Homer, Kenai, Fort Yukon and Venetie, all of them. Cordova, Whittier, St. Mary's, King Salmon, Petersburg, Palmer, Wasilla, Anaktuvuk Pass, Circle, Eagle, Paxson are some more places I've flown, but I can't remember them all. There have been so many going back to the 1960s.

I didn't make any water landings, though. I've never been on floats. Once I flew around from village to village with the bishop of the Alaska Diocese. He was stopping in at the churches. That took me to a lot of places.

I gave a lot of rides to tourists who wanted to see the scenery. Sometimes they got scared because they didn't know what they were in for. Once I had to land and let somebody out who was feeling sick, but mostly it was because she—it was a woman—was scared. I had to take her back down.

There were a few times that people barfed. The panic thing is a little worrisome. When a lady in the back seat says, "Hey, you're much too close to the mountain, we're going to hit, we're going to crash," that can make you nervous. Some people have never been in mountain country before. They don't understand the distance you are from the peak or from a ledge. It looks like you're right on top of it. You're not because the scale is so enormous. I had that happen a few times. They'd never been up in anything but a big jet. Once, I turned around to tell the passengers something and this woman in the back said, "Now, Mr. Thomas, will you please turn around and mind your own business."

I learned to be very careful and not get too close to any place that would make somebody panicky. You don't want anyone who is in a panic. They might try to grab the controls or do something crazy.

TAY: Once, even our granddaughter got scared on the way back from Camp Denali.

She was holding my knee the whole time. At one point she grabbed my hand. She was very nervous.

LOWELL: I never had a walkup client who was famous who decided on the spur of the moment that they wanted to take a flight, but I gave rides to Eunice Kennedy Shriver, who was involved in founding the Special Olympics, Walter Cronkite, and Charles Lindbergh. But I think we knew they were coming. They didn't just walk up and have me say, "Hey, you're Walter Cronkite." Lindbergh kicked the tires and walked around and inspected the plane. Old pilot. Some people came and said they were from New York and they knew my father or my family. There were quite a few of those.

So many people just want to see as much of Alaska as they can. But really aviation has been essential to Alaska from the beginning when airplanes were able to fly in the north. It would be hard to get along without aviation in Alaska because the distances are so vast,

At home in the pilot's seat in a plane, Lowell Thomas Jr. flew more than a million miles.

there are so few roads, and just one railroad. So aviation is the ticket, the way to get around, ever since flying machines were safe enough to take to the air. Aviation is woven into Alaska's history and it is the flying-est of all the states. I know over the years I heard Alaska was number one per capita in the number of pilots and I think we're still number one. It comes to mind that something like one in seven people in Alaska is a licensed pilot.

There are so many communities in the Interior and up north that would otherwise be inaccessible without airplanes. But there are also a lot of opportunities to just go and land on a gravel bar someplace to go fishing. Other areas there are no prepared landing spots at all. You just go find your own place, or clear a spot in advance before you bring your plane in. I've gone someplace and built my own strip, clearing rocks out of the way so I could get in. I did it in Bahrain, but that was somewhere else. In Alaska I did it on the west shore of Cook Inlet.

I flew in and once I got there I cleared out the area so I would be able to fly in more safely the next time.

You used to feel like you were pioneering a bit. You landed on some places among the mountains where no one had ever been before. It's always kind of fun to do that. There were no structures, no people, no telephone lines. There was nothing and nobody. It almost made you feel as if you had traveled through time.

I was always excited about aviation and got the bug from those early heroes of mine like Jimmy Doolittle and Eddie Rickenbacker, but I think flying in Alaska is even better because of the wide-open spaces. There are not as many radio aids to navigation. That was certainly true in the early years that I was doing it. It's a little better now because you can fly with a GPS and always know exactly where you are. But before that you had to be really careful about watching where you were on the map and not losing track of where you were going. Physical landmarks were important, more so than in other places, because there were not many other aids. I'd do it all of the time looking out the window for physical landmarks. You had to or you could get lost in a hurry, especially if visibility got bad. It was terribly important to know where you were at every moment.

Alaska had a lot of great pilots. I met Noel Wien. I knew Bob Reeve quite well. He was a great fellow. He had lots of stories and a good sense of humor. The Anchorage Glacier Pilots baseball team was named after Bob Reeve. And Ray Peterson. I've lost track of some of them. Before GPS we had to make do with less technology. Radio was the most important, radio range. Let's say there are four areas and there's a dit-dot A in one area and an N in another. The beam was right where the two came together. If you got the dit-dot and the dit-dot you were right on the beam and it would take you right to the transmitting station. That was an early form of navigating and getting around. It was automatic. Every hour at a certain time they would come on and somebody would broadcast the local weather at that particular location.

Then the ADF, the Automatic Direction Finder, came along. You could actually tune in a radio station and hone in on it. There was a

Tay (left), Anne, her parents, the Pryors, fellow pilot Ray Peterson, and son David on the right.

needle that would swing and pick up the point right at the station if you were close enough and if a thunderstorm wasn't pulling the needle off in some direction.

Those were the early ways of getting around if you weren't just using a map and looking out the window physically. Regardless of those radio things, you wanted to have a map and verify it. Sometimes those radio waves could be off a little bit, mislead you by getting a bounce off a mountain. That tended to throw the ADF needle in the wrong direction. It must have been very hard for those guys in the early days, especially in the dark, or when visibility was poor, and if they didn't have good maps. It would be a pretty tricky business I would say.

Even with technology improving we still fly that way, using a map. That's the basic. Just keep an eye on where the hell you are. Mark where you are on a river and where the mountains are. There was a pretty good camaraderie among the pilots. There weren't as many when I got to Alaska in the sixties as there are now, but you got to know the others pretty well. We didn't have any big organization to get together and have drinks together and stuff like that, but some of them had a reputation and you'd sort of get together one-on-one with fellows who were flying the same routes for the same reason.

Pilots got well-known for being successful, doing a good job, and not cracking up. They stayed out of trouble and were able to complete their missions getting people where they wanted to go. Some got to be known because they carried sled dogs and a famous musher or something. They carried sled dogs here and there in the back of the airplane. I never did that. I never got involved in flying with the Iditarod Trail. I flew a few dogs sometimes to someone who needed some help getting somewhere. I probably should have made a sled-dog film, but I never did.

The early pilots were pioneers in delivering the mail. There were some wonderful stories about flying the mail, persevering to get through regardless of the odds. Guys took some real chances in those days. I didn't feel as if I missed out. I saw enough tough flying. Plenty of that. If you flew enough miles even the best pilots had problems. If it happened you didn't really want to talk about it. I'm sure they had some forced landings and some crack-ups too. I remember Don Sheldon had crack-ups, but he didn't talk about it.

I calculate that I had five major forced landings in my career, from the military to traveling long distance, to Alaska. In November of 1964, the same year as the Good Friday Earthquake, I landed on the Nenana Highway while traveling with Jim Binkley. That was the family that ran the Riverboat Discovery in Fairbanks.

We had gone out to Nulato (there's another community on my life list) on the Yukon River because I had agreed to be the Republican candidate for Congress. Alaska has just one Congressman for the state because of its population. I ended up losing to Ralph Rivers.

Jim was my northern campaign manager. We noted that the election return was like 180 votes for Rivers and something like three votes for Thomas. We thought surely there had been some hanky-panky and we flew there to interview some folks looking for evidence that would help us get the election results thrown out and a new election called.

We landed on river ice with the plane's skis down and walked up to the village. We found only a few kids and old folks there. None of them had anything to say about the election. I don't know where everyone else was, but we left disappointed.

It was very cold and I had thrown a sleeping bag over the engine for extra warmth. We weren't there long enough for it to cool off much anyway. Off we went. The gas tanks were full out of Fairbanks. The total trip out and back should have taken about three hours and forty-five minutes and that would be no problem with four hours and thirty minutes of fuel. But after three hours and thirty minutes, just coming up on the hills west of Fairbanks, the engine sputtered and began to fade.

I switched tanks to one I thought I had already emptied. The engine picked up briefly, and then began to fade again. How could both tanks be dry? There was no question that we were looking at a forced landing. We were coming over Chena Ridge and it was nearly dark. I was looking frantically for a place to get down. The best bet was somewhere on the Nenana Highway where it zigzagged up the Chena River. There was an uphill straightaway off to the left and trees on the near side of it. I headed for that area, watching the air speed carefully, knowing that stretching into a glide is often fatal.

On with the landing lights in order to see the treetops. Jim was as quiet as a mouse. There was a tight turn left to stay over the road and then a right around a curve. I just missed a road sign with the left wing. I leveled out and we landed on the straightaway. I had to hold the brakes to keep from rolling back on the hill.

Jim and I jumped out and knelt to kiss the pavement. We looked at the engine to see why we ran out of fuel and we noticed a reddish gas stain on the top of the fuselage emanating from a small hole in the back of the gooseneck air tank intake. At least fifteen gallons must have been siphoned out of there. But why? Climbing up on the left wheel and strut I found that the little neoprene ball that runs in the gooseneck to block gas vapors from escaping on the ground had frozen into the closed position. Later I learned it was caused by vapors from the Yukon River while the plane was parked on the ice.

While Jim and I caught our breath we heard a truck approaching. I got out the plane's flashlight and waved the beam to warn the trucker. He pulled over, a little dumbfounded. But then he was most helpful pushing the plane off the road and into the weeds where it spent the night. I had called the control tower in Fairbanks and before long a state police patrol car came out, checked the scene, and drove us to town.

The next morning I returned with two, five-gallon cans of fuel, poured them in, started up, and while a trooper stood by to block traffic I took off for the Fairbanks airport. When the incident made statewide news folks said, "Why didn't you do that before the election? It could have made the difference."

Probably not in Nulato, though.

19

Around the World
a New Way

In 1965, Lowell Thomas Jr. took part in a unique journey that marked a first in aviation—an American expedition designed to fly around the earth. For the first time, an airplane was going to attempt to complete the adventure longitudinally, between the poles.

For many years Lowell Thomas Sr. had been an advocate of such an enticing operation, but technology had not yet caught up to the conditions that flyers would face. By the middle of the sixties, however, the conditions were ripe. It had become possible for a jet to realistically make the hop from the North Pole to the South Pole quickly and safely.

Lowell Sr. had claimed that the trip between the poles would be "the last great exploration of the earth by conventional aircraft." By 1965, when such a prospect became reality he was seventy-three years old and did not consider himself fit for such a journey.

So it was that on November 14, 1965, it was Lowell Thomas Jr., not his father, broadcasting on the CBS Radio Network from a jet plane named the *Polecat* that was flying at thirty-one thousand feet above the Pacific Ocean. The objective of the plane and its crew was to become the first plane to fly around the world from north to south, from the North Pole to the South Pole.

The journey—and another Lowell Thomas Jr. adventure—began in Palm Springs, California, a few hours earlier on the same day. Next would be a stop in Honolulu, the official jumping-off spot for the flight. Lowell Jr. described it as "the last great flight yet to be made on this planet, a double pole flight never before attempted."

Pilots Fred Austin and Harrison Finch, who worked for TWA, hatched the scheme and took a leave of absence from their jobs to see if they could capture the prize. In a rapidly shrinking world there were almost no more firsts to be claimed in the world of exploration, but this was one. Colonel Willard Rockwell, chairman of the board of Rockwell-Standard Corporation of Pittsburgh, stepped up to fund the project.

As fevered preparations were made to get the plane off the ground, it was noted that the *Polecat* had a range of eight thousand miles at six hundred miles an hour. Lowell Jr. was in California for the start of the flight, but ironically, after taking off from Hawaii the *Polecat* was going to fly over Alaska and over the Arctic Ocean to the North Pole.

❖ ❖ ❖

LOWELL: The primary reason why no around-the-world flight by way of the two poles was never made until 1965 was because up until then planes did not have enough range to make it a safe proposition. In the old days it would have been virtually impossible, if not downright foolish, to attempt such a flight. Now there was a Boeing 707 available that should be up to the task.

As far as my being on the flight, it was really a stroke of luck. I happened to be in the Los Angeles area on a speaking tour when word came that I could go along as official historian. I climbed on board in a hurry. The man who should have been on the *Polecat* was really my father, because he was the official historian of the first flight around the world of any type—the global flight of 1924.

It took six months for those Army flyers to complete the journey. Our schedule called for making the trip in three days. There were forty people aboard the *Polecat*. That included five pilots, three flight engineers, three navigators, and a communication man with an assistant and several editors, writers, cameramen, and newsmen. There were also a multitude of observers, including Colonel Rockwell, whose firm had made a two hundred thousand dollar financial grant to the project. Because of his largesse, the official name of the trip became "The Rockwell Polar Flight." Also included was Bernt Balchen, the explorer who had been the first man to pilot a plane over both poles. Fred Austin and Harrison Finch, who dreamed up the trip in the first place, were the flight commanders.

One qualification for the five pilots was that they have experience with zero ceiling and zero visibility, if conditions deteriorated. The two trip originators and the other three pilots took turns at the controls. The other pilots for this historic flight were J. L. (Jack) Martin, Robert N. Buck, and James R. Gannett.

When we left California and set out for Honolulu we ran into strong headwinds and that kept our speed down to 420 miles an hour. We were also up in the jet stream and that was not helping. I issued periodic broadcasts from the flight to update our listeners whenever it was practical or when I had something to say.

Reaching Honolulu we climbed down from the plane and were greeted by a couple of eye-catching Hawaiian girls who came forward with the usual assortment of leis and kisses. Back in 1924 the Army fliers had trouble finding an Eskimo to rub noses with when they made their first landing. When we set off for the North Pole we were still wearing our leis and nourishing a large bunch of fresh tropical flowers. It was November 14 by the Hawaiian calendar, but it was already 5:54 A.M. Greenwich Mean Time on Monday, November 15. Greenwich Mean Time was our official reference time guideline for the flight.

Upon leaving Hawaii we climbed to thirty-two thousand feet, on our way to the North Pole before turning and landing in London. The North Pole is defined as the point in the Northern Hemisphere where the Earth's axis of rotation meets its surface. That is where all lines of longitude meet. The North Pole is covered with snow and ice, but that snow and ice does not cover land, it covers the deep sea of the Arctic Ocean. The depth of the water at the North Pole is somewhere between thirteen thousand and fourteen thousand feet. Both the United States and the Soviet Union sent submarines to measure the depth at different times. While normally someone skis to the pole or makes it to the pole by dog team, they are not standing on land. The closest permanent body of land is estimated to be in Greenland about four hundred-plus miles away. The closest land that is inhabited is the village of Alert Bay in the Canadian province of Nunavut about five hundred miles away.

I took note on the air when we passed over Anchorage. I hoped that the local radio station KFQD would pick up my talk. I said I was sorry that I couldn't stop in to say hello to Tay and the children. Including my lectures and this flight I had been away from home for a month. "I'll have to continue on around the world before returning home," I said. "But tell my wife that I'll try to talk to her on the radio some time later as we fly southward over the Atlantic. Did you get that, KFQD?"

As we flew north we passed not far from Barrow, Alaska, the northernmost settlement in North America, and even closer to the whaling community of Wainwright. At that point we were at thirty-seven thousand feet. While in that vicinity a minor scent of smoke was detected in the plane. Speculation was that there was an electrical problem. Any type of problem could become serious where we were headed and could cause us to abort our mission. However, within a few minutes the trouble was pinpointed. A ventilator fan motor had burned up.

I was on the air broadcasting from thirty-five thousand feet as our navigators informed us we were above the North Pole. "Flash!" I said. "It's about 2:30 P.M. and word is that we're over the North Pole right now. We still can't see any of the ice pack because of the undercast. Almost everybody is up in the forward cabin. There's a little ceremony in progress as we fly over the Ultimate North."

A little bit later, after passing over the North Pole, we had the unusual experience of seeing both a sunrise and a sunset within only about an hour of each other.

This was the only time I ever visited the North Pole. It was not as if we could land and take a walk around. That would have been pretty exciting. So the most anyone saw in the area was snow and ice.

We barely slowed down over the pole and kept on flying at high speed. When we landed at Greenwich Mean Time at Heathrow Airport in London it was 7:48 P.M. We made the 7,413-mile flight from Honolulu over the North Pole to London in thirteen hours and fifty-four minutes. We were at Heathrow, where we took on ten thousand gallons of fuel, for a little less than three hours.

We also had to take on fuel in Lisbon, Portugal. It took just two hours and nineteen minutes to get there, establishing a new transport speed record. In all, during the flight the plane set eight transport speed records. Resuming flight, we headed for the coast of Africa. All of us got a little bit of sleep at different times during the flight despite the temptation to try and stay up indefinitely or all of the way through. Nobody wanted to miss anything exciting, but we were traveling around the clock.

Rather remarkably, when you think of the limited technology we had when we were flying *Charlie* around the world in the mid-1950s, I was able to speak directly with Tay in Anchorage via two-way radio. We talked through the Collins Radio control station in Cedar Rapids, Iowa, where they made a phone patch. Our conversation was pretty simple. I asked if she could hear me and she said she could. I told her that we were above the South Atlantic, about halfway between Lisbon and Buenos Aires. Tay said that they were thinking of me at home and listening to the radio all day to hear the reports. I was actually able to speak to my daughter, Anne, too.

The Argentine skies were clear and the temperature was eighty-nine degrees as Jack Martin brought the plane in to land at Buenos Aires where government officials were waiting to greet us. We flew the 5,957 miles from Lisbon in eleven hours and fifty-six minutes, which was another speed record.

We were on the ground for about three hours. Bernt Balchen soaked up the sunshine. He was about to return to the scene of one of his great early triumphs. In the early 1930s he was the pilot who flew explorer Lincoln Ellsworth in the Antarctic. I took to the airwaves again after leaving Buenos Aires, reporting in four thousand miles from the South Pole.

An hour out of Buenos Aires I was able to conduct another conversation, this time with my father sitting at his desk in New York. It was a surprise conversation. "When you fly over the Antarctic Peninsula, I don't want anybody to go out of their way, but if you could get a look at those L.T. Mountains named for me by Finn Ronne, it would be kind of fun because I've never seen them. So it's up to you." They were actually the Lowell Thomas Mountains, but my father referred to himself as L.T. Ronne made nine expeditions to Antarctica and named this group of mountains after Dad on his 1946–48 expedition.

I informed Dad that we were going to try to sneak over and take a look, but as is always the case in Antarctica, it would depend on the weather. Not long after I talked with L.T. Sr. we passed over the first icebergs and reached the outer limits of the Antarctic continent. But a cloud cover developed beneath us and we could see none of the icy terrain. We had to abandon our plans to get a look at those mountains. As we sped over the ice fields we sent a message to President Lyndon Johnson in Washington.

Shortly after passing the Antarctic Peninsula and reaching the main coastline itself, the clouds rolled back and the visibility was unlimited. We approached the South Pole at 550 miles an hour. I went back on the air for a report. "Hello, everyone, this is Lowell Thomas Jr. reporting from the *Polecat*—over the South Pole at this very moment. We've just completed the first historic flight from the North to the South Pole. Our altitude is thirty-seven thousand feet and we're in bright sunshine over the US Amundsen-Scott Station."

We were verbally assisted to the pole by one of the forty men stationed there. All five pilots took a quick turn at the controls. It was a moment to be remembered. Again, like the North Pole, this was my only visit to the South Pole. Unlike the North Pole, the South Pole is actually part of a continent, not merely over water. The first humans to reach the South Pole were led by Norwegian Roald Amundsen in

December of 1911. His party beat English explorer Robert Falcon Scott's expedition to the site by a mere thirty-four days.

After we passed above the pole—again it would have been a terrific thing if we could have landed and walked there—I had another conversation with my father in New York. "It's great to know that things are going OK," he said.

After we landed in New Zealand and took off again I had a third conversation with L.T. Sr. "Our flight is almost over and so far we've survived the dangers and hazards that our early aviators face on their great flights from point-to-point." We chatted a little and he said, "It's been a great flight and I'm looking forward to seeing you soon. So long."

I am quite sure that if he could have been with us on the flight my father would have been there. I don't recall exactly why he was not, but it was probably simply age at that point in his life.

In all, we traveled 26,230 miles in the *Polecat*, flying over both poles in a record sixty-two hours, twenty-seven minutes, thirty-five seconds. That included layovers. The actual time in flight was fifty-one hours, twenty-seven minutes. When they mapped out the expedition, Austin and Harrison had predicted that fifty-two hours of flying time would be required to complete the mission.

At the end of that journey I believed that the record flight over the North Pole and South Pole would stand as a thrill of a lifetime for everyone involved. So many years later—and it was almost fifty years ago—I can say that journey was one of the high points of my life.

20

Politics and Conservation

When Lowell Thomas Jr. was invited to become the Republican Party candidate for Congress in 1962 he discovered that he liked politics and thought it was worth a try to get elected. He lost, but gave it another, more serious whirl chasing the same office in 1964.

Also on Thomas's mind, the longer he lived in Alaska, were environmental issues. When the United States bought Alaska from Russia in 1867 for $7.2 million with Secretary of State William H. Seward as the main agent representing the country in the exchange, many dismissed the deal as Seward's Folly.

That description was likely forgotten when the Alaska Gold Rush began in 1898. It was further relegated to the back burner when Americans realized that Alaska was a source of a potential jackpot of oil wealth.

Suddenly, cold, out-of-the-way Alaska seemed as if it might be worth a whole bunch more than people gave it credit for. While the oil boom, and the famous Trans-Alaska Pipeline's construction and opening in 1976, burnished Alaska's image for some, the new mineral wealth posed a threat to environmentalists concerned about what would happen to the state's pristine lands.

Many believed that Alaska was the most beautiful place on earth—Lowell Thomas among them—and wished to see the spectacular land preserved for future generations. Thomas did not move to Alaska with the eye of a corporate executive trying to see how much profit he could wring from the land. He and his family moved to Alaska because they thought it was a special place, yes indeed the Last Frontier, and they did not wish to see it ruined.

Thomas ended up spending eight years serving in the Alaska state legislature and then a four-year term as lieutenant governor as part of Jay Hammond's gubernatorial administration. The Hammond administration's greatest, and most enduring accomplishment in many minds, was the creation of the Alaska Permanent Dividend Fund, rewarding residents with annual payments stemming from a trust fund fueled by oil industry profits. Or as people who live in the Lower 48 states often say, "You mean they give you money just for living there?"

❖ ❖ ❖

LOWELL: A lot of people knew my name and some of that was a residual benefit from my father's name. I thought it would be easier to get into Congress from Alaska than it would from New York, New Jersey, or Pennsylvania.

While I did not win my first Congressional race, I had invested enough time in campaigning and speaking politically that I wanted to stay with it and pursue it a little bit more. I didn't want to totally quit. After twice losing for Congress I decided to run for the state legislature. In my mind the main issues revolved around conservation versus development. I felt very strongly about it. I didn't want to see Alaska turned into another New Jersey.

We liked the wilderness and we wanted to protect it as much as possible, and the wildlife, and the native people. Those were my primary concerns. Alaska was a young state. There was a lot to do and you could make a difference. I put a lot of my focus on creating state parks and I think I was instrumental in getting Chugach State Park established.

In 1974, Lowell was elected lieutenant governor of Alaska. Here he is campaigning with Jay Hammond, who won the governorship in Soldotna. With them are Diana Tillion and Bob Palmer.

I spent nearly eight years in the state senate—two terms of four years each—after being elected in 1966. I'm not sure what made me want to be a politician. Maybe it was a substitute for joining the Foreign Service. I had taken those international government courses at Princeton. It just seemed to be a field that I had some basic groundwork in. I was enticed to run because I had a good, famous name, and you always know that's going to be helpful getting votes. After I lost in the run for Congress I thought, "Hell, I'd like to do something." The thing I should have done in the beginning was run for the legislature and then think about Congress. I kind of got to thinking I didn't really want to move to Washington, so in a way I was glad I lost.

Jay Hammond was in the senate at the same time I was and he had some of the same interests as I did. We struck it off right away. He felt strongly about protecting the environment as well as developing

A Thomas family camping trip in the early 1960s.

things. We both believed that balance had to be very carefully handled and I thought it was encouraging that sort of spirit was still there.

TAY: When Lowell was in the legislature I stayed in Anchorage with the kids. They were in school. The legislature always started in January and ended in the spring. We didn't want to move the kids out of their regular schools. Maybe if they had been younger things would have been different. They were both getting active in things like cross-country skiing. Having the plane made things easier. Lowell flew back on Friday nights for long weekends and then went back to Juneau.

LOWELL: There were a lot Alaskans who believed in maintaining Alaska, but there were others, on the other hand, who were pushing awfully hard just to get the development going. They wanted to mine and cut down trees. The same thing keeps going on today. I just felt I was in a very good spot to try to do something about it. I felt preservation was important and was needed. I thought I could contribute to conservation and I spoke about it often. I became known for that. I also spoke about trying to save wolves in terms of getting the bounty off of hunting them. It seems as if it is still an issue more than forty years later. Some of these issues never stop. They never go away.

One time we had Charles Lindbergh come to Juneau and he spoke to a joint session of the legislature about how it was inhuman to use aircraft to pursue wildlife, to shoot any creature from the air.

At that time, before the pipeline, Alaska was not a wealthy state. That was one of the concerns of people who were opposed to statehood. They said Alaska was going to become a ward of the federal government. The oil money changed that idea very drastically. There was no Permanent Fund yet so we were feeling our way as a new state trying to take care of business. We didn't want to leave management of the state or management of the pipeline to the federal government. We wanted the state to get into it and be sure it was done in a way that would be as safe as possible. That was the huge issue of development versus conservation in terms of the future of the environment.

Jay Hammond worked very hard on that and I was with him on that one all the way through. We really had to work like the devil on that. We wanted Alaska to get our fair share of the oil money and how taxes were applied to the oil companies was a very big issue.

TAY: At the time Lowell was a Republican, but more often than not he was working with the Democrats and voting with the Democrats, so there were a lot of splits on things.

LOWELL: This was a time when Alaska was a young state and the legislature was basically deciding by its actions what kind of state it was going to be. It was on my priority list to preserve this place for future generations, but the developers thought that's what they were doing too, only in a different way.

The big thing was getting Chugach State Park established. I don't know if it is my greatest accomplishment, but I am very proud of my work on that. My name was on the bill and now I live on the Anchorage

Hillside just down the street from an entrance to the park. A lot of other people worked very hard on it too, and they asked me if I would carry the bill as the primary sponsor. I was happy to do it. But there were a lot of other people like Walter Parker and others who had been hiking there and wanted to save it. They got behind it in a big way.

I am very proud of having a hand in that. People were going to go in there and look for minerals. That was the threat if we didn't preserve it. That was a great concern. The mining community was mad at us. They said, "Hey, don't do that. Don't lock it up. That's pretty valuable country up there, we think." They thought we were crazy people. They thought we were all crazy guys blocking progress. You hear it all the time. It's constant—blocking progress. In most places it's build another subdivision or save those trees. Oh, and "Don't try to save the polar bears. Hell, there are minerals up there. Don't lock it up." It's the old story.

Chugach State Park has more than 495,000 acres and as people know the eastern horizon of Anchorage is the Chugach Mountain Range. The park begins right there, just up the hillside in the middle of the homes that have been built there since. It's all wilderness back there for miles. I don't know what kind of development there might have been otherwise, but with the mountains, the wild and the rugged terrain back there it just made sense to make sure it was preserved. Chugach State Park is the third biggest state park in the country. One of the big things is how accessible it is to the city. You can be driving on the Seward Highway and ten minutes later be in the park. I think it's one of the best things we ever did while I was in the legislature.

Some of us founded the Chugach State Park Ad Hoc Committee that brought attention to the need to keep the area clear of development. Some of the other people on that committee were the mountain climber Art Davidson, Rep. Helen Beirne, and several other citizens. The bill to create Chugach State Park was signed into law by Governor Keith Miller in 1970. I remember when the Anchorage Assembly passed a resolution congratulating those of us who were on the committee on the fortieth anniversary of the founding of the park.

That was something that I was known for and in 2001 I received the first Bruce F. Vento Award from the National Park Trust and I was very proud of that recognition. It was a lifetime achievement award named after a Minnesota congressman who died. They had a nice ceremony in Anchorage. A lot of people came from around the country. The award was very nice, a large, round silver item and at the ceremony I was recognized for really doing what I thought was the right thing to do.

In 2004 I was inducted into the Alaska Conservation Hall of Fame. Over the years I have helped out a lot of groups that I thought were doing good work for the environment, including the National Parks Conservation Association and the Alaska Conservation Foundation. I didn't do it for recognition, but because I thought they were doing important work to preserve and protect Alaska and that's how I thought.

In 2000 I made a $1 million donation to the Alaska Conservation Foundation. It just felt very good at that point of my life to be able to do something like that.

After getting elected to the legislature in 1966 and staying in until 1974, I had had enough. I didn't really enjoy the schmoozing scene in Juneau after hours. There was always the cocktail hour and a lot of drinking. People were making deals in the bars and negotiating and I wasn't really part of that. I just wanted to do my work and go to bed early.

There were some suggestions that I run for the United States Senate, but I didn't want to do that. After I lost the race for Congress I realized I didn't want to move to Washington, D.C. anyway, so it was easy to say forget it about that. There were even some people saying I should run for governor. I really didn't want to do that either. At that point I just wanted to go home to Anchorage and head for the hills, get out in the mountains and the wilderness. That's where my real love was. At that point the sooner I could get out of Juneau the better was how I felt.

Jay Hammond had decided to run for governor and he wanted me to join him on the ticket for lieutenant governor. I didn't want Wally Hickel to be elected, but I really didn't want to run. Jay talked me into it. Jay was a bush figure. He was very well-known in the outlying areas, but my base was in the more populated areas. I pulled in votes in Anchorage and Juneau. Jay asked me if I would consider doing it and I decided to go ahead. I had to be persuaded and one of the things that convinced me was who it looked like would be governor if Jay wasn't going to be.

Bill Egan was on the way out. He had been governor in two different blocks of time and 1974 was his last year. We worked hard campaigning. I put a lot of miles on my plane campaigning. Running for lieutenant governor was one thing that got me out to a lot of Alaska communities. In a state like Alaska having your own plane can be a big advantage. I flew the Helio Courier all over between the spread-out villages.

Hammond was such a good cause that I had to jump in with both feet. Tay was definitely a big influence. She had worked hard on my elections. The cause was to elect a governor who cared deeply about Alaska's natural wilderness values and make sure that they not be trampled by the developmental stampede already underway. Jay's goals matched mine, to slow things down a bit in order to determine what was and wasn't beneficial to the state and to determine what steps government should take to minimize environmental damage. Jay was going to create an Alaska Growth Policy Council to be chaired by the new lieutenant governor.

This was a very close race and the fact that I could get around to a lot of places probably helped. You wonder if having the Helio Courier actually tipped the balance in the vote. I think my ability to get to a lot of those rural places outside of the bigger cities had something to do with the vote and us winning. Jay flew with me several times, so we both appeared in these villages.

TAY: Many years later when we had dinner with Tony Knowles, after he had been governor, he told us that someone he knew offered to fly him anywhere he wanted to go in the state and that would be his contribution towards the campaign. Tony thought that helped a great deal.

LOWELL: We were long shots to be elected when we started out. We had a tiny, little log cabin downtown that was our campaign headquarters. We went door to door and village to village. The hard work paid off.

TAY: Believe it or not I was the campaign manager for Anchorage. I worked with a state senator from Kenai, Bob Palmer, and a well-known public relations man. We were very low budget to start with. By the time election night rolled around and we were watching the results come in we were pretty confident. At the end we thought we had won.

LOWELL: Jay was initially ill-at-ease with public speaking, but he did a superb job explaining his goals, always modest, using humor. Alaskans saw him as something of a Daniel Boone or Davy Crockett, a frontiersman, a true Alaskan.

   During that campaign a columnist in the *Anchorage Times* wrote of me, "Soft-spoken, concerned and sincere, Thomas seems far removed from the body-punching, go-for-the-throat school of American politics. Although he is not above taking a shot at an opponent, the slight-graying Thomas does so with a seeming reluctance that borders on distaste for the necessity of doing so. The impression he leaves is that of a headmaster or statesman removed from the crush of political battle to a realm where he can balance the good and bad with little concern for political consideration."

   People wondered why I didn't run for governor, believing my chances of success were greater than Hammond's. I said I had a lot of respect for him and agreed with his honest approach. How important did I consider the office of lieutenant governor? Not very, kind of like a car's spare tire.

   Jay finished first in the primary, ahead of Wally Hickel and Keith Miller, who had succeeded Hickel when he left the office to join the Nixon cabinet. I cleaned up in the lieutenant governor's race, winning by more than fifteen thousand votes.

   Stumping around Alaska became even more frantic. We were running against incumbent Bill Egan and Red Boucher, the former mayor of Fairbanks who had founded the Alaska Goldpanners baseball team and the Alaska Baseball League. Right up to the November elections, whenever I spoke to groups, or to the media, I emphasized our concern with protecting and enhancing Alaska's renewable resources.

On election day Jay and I were declared the winners by 287 votes. Even after an immediate recount we won by one half of one percent, or 365 votes. And then there was another recount. The *final* final margin was 490 votes.

So in 1974 I became lieutenant governor. Since we knew I was going to be there for four years we bought a house in Juneau. It was on Douglas Island, just across the bridge from Juneau. It was a little A-frame. It seemed as if they put it up in like five days or something and then we finished it off ourselves. It was a quiet little spot just outside of Juneau.

During that term, in 1977, oil began to flow through the Trans-Alaska Pipeline from Prudhoe Bay to Valdez. The Permanent Fund to prevent the state from squandering all of the oil money it earned and the program was approved by the legislature in 1976 and began paying dividends to residents of the state in the early 1980s. That has always been viewed as the signature achievement of the Jay Hammond gubernatorial administration. After one term as lieutenant governor I was happy to leave Juneau and return to Anchorage. That was the end of my career in elective politics and I was content with that.

21

Passion for Skiing

One of the great passions of Lowell Thomas's life has been skiing. That probably foreshadowed his living in a place like Alaska that is known for its snow, but while Alaska is a cross-country skier's paradise, it is less renowned for downhill skiing. That means that Thomas has pursued the opportunity to downhill ski in several places around the United States.

However, cross-country skiing has also remained close to his heart and he has participated in that activity in the way it was first intended—as transportation in back country areas—rather than as competitive sport. Skiing is Thomas's favorite sport to participate in. In his mind it ranks far above spectator sports such as football and basketball.

Thomas learned to ski at a very young age because skiing was also a passion of his father. Lowell Sr. made appearances on downhill slopes wherever possible and even worked hard to develop some of those areas. Lowell Jr. also loved skiing whenever he could fit it into his schedule and became a member of the ski team at Dartmouth College.

Much later in life Thomas worked with other Alaskans to develop ski opportunities and he became a major contributor to the creation of the Alaska Methodist University ski team. The small, private, Anchorage-based college is now known as Alaska Pacific University, and APU runs a world-class club program. Thomas provided a $1 million donation to the establishment of the APU Nordic Ski Center in 1999 and it is now a regional Olympic training center. Some members of the United States National Team and Olympic team are connected to the program. Among those representing the program are world champion cross-country skier Kikkan Randall of Anchorage and Olympians Holly Brooks and James Southam. All three have won US national championships.

❖ ❖ ❖

LOWELL: Skiing has always been a big part of my life. My father taught me to ski when I was very young, maybe seven years old, and I have always loved it, even after I broke an ankle when I was ten or eleven years old. We always took a lot of family vacations that were tied in to visiting ski slopes in the northeastern part of the country, and also in Colorado.

It always took a little bit of an effort to get someplace where you could ski, but there were places in New York and in New England that were not too far away. We even went skiing in Arizona. Nobody associates snow with Arizona, but there are places located at pretty high altitude and people ski in the Superstition Mountains outside of Flagstaff. There are ten-thousand-foot peaks there. You can be skiing amongst the trees. People just don't know about the mountains they have there. They think of the desert and the heat first.

Then at Dartmouth they had a ski team, which I joined. That's when I took up ski jumping too. Throughout my life most of my skiing was downhill, but being in Alaska there were many chances to go cross-country skiing in the back country. Many times when I parked my plane somewhere I would strap on the skis and go exploring.

Ski jumping is one of those activities where people think you are a little bit crazy to try it. It seems in this country they only pay attention to it once every four years when the Olympics is happening. There aren't very many ski jumping facilities in the United States either, so you really have to want to do it. It's not an easy sport either. I had to work pretty hard to get any good at it.

If you are living in Anchorage, there are basically two places nearby where over the years you could go downhill skiing. There's Alyeska in Girdwood, which is very popular, and when I was skiing often there was Arctic Valley. We went to Arctic Valley a lot with the kids. They have had World Cup races at Alyeska, but Arctic Valley was a good place to start kids skiing. We got Anne and Dave started doing both cross-country, which they had at school, and doing downhill at Arctic Valley.

I got involved with the Alaska Methodist University ski team before they changed the name of the school to Alaska Pacific University. I knew the coach, Jim Mahaffey, and he persuaded me to come over and help out a little bit. I was familiar with an ice field in the Chugach Mountains and we decided to fly some of the athletes there for training purposes. You were never going to be short of snow there. I was really just helping out, but I sort of became an assistant coach/pilot for the team.

That probably made me the only ski team pilot in the United States. But where we went, there was no facility whatsoever like a warming hut or building where you could put your skis on. What was needed was some kind of shelter where people could spend the night.

We decided to build one ourselves. A couple of new coaches did the hard labor, I think, and I did a little bit of shoveling. I did make a pretty hefty donation to pay for the whole thing. Mostly I just wanted to help them out and I flew them in and out so the kids would have a good training location. This all goes way back. I think it was the 1960s. Sven Johansson, who was a great skier and has a race named after him in Anchorage, was still alive and skiing. Then my daughter, Anne, got into it.

TAY: Anne became a very good skier. She was one of the top women cross-country skiers in the country. She almost made the Olympic

Tay involved in the cooking for thirty people at the opening of the Alaska Methodist/Alaska Pacific mountain house in 1967.

team. She came within one place of it. Anne played a big role in going up to the training area with Lowell with her ski friends and the ski team.

LOWELL: When I flew skiers in there I brought my skis and did a lot of cross-country skiing. That connection to Alaska Pacific goes back a long time. Every year they come to the house for a party and spend some time with us.

TAY: They won't let me cook. They bring all of the food and cook it. They say they don't want to be a burden, so we have a lot of pictures of the skiers wearing aprons. They actually brought the things that they had cooked. One of the men made bread and another made casseroles. They do keep in touch with us. It means a lot to me and Lowell. Then when we hear what they accomplish we can put a face to the name.

Kikkan (Randall) has been the biggest star. It certainly gives us a rooting interest when we watch the Winter Olympics on TV. She is something. She's unbelievable. Four times on the Olympic team, a world champion. But you know what she did most of the time when she came here last time? She spent most of the time playing with Jack, our cat.

LOWELL: Besides the time flying the young people into the Chugach Range I used to fly myself and friends to glaciers and other areas so we could do some back country skiing. There are so many places you can go in Alaska with a plane on skis where you would otherwise never get to.

Sometimes we flew to the lower part of the Alaska Range. I'd go with Paul Crews Sr., Rodman Wilson, John Gardi, and George Wichman. We all loved skiing, the wilderness, and being out in nature and surrounded by mountains. George climbed a lot of Alaska mountains. We all had an interest in climbing and some of the mountains were ones nobody had ever climbed before. I'd take the plane and a couple of the guys and we would case the scene from the air. Then we would drop down and land to determine if the mountain was suitable for a climb.

We did that quite often. We got to know one another through skiing and the Alaska Mountaineering Club. In the early sixties I made a film—nobody commissioned it—that was part of my lecture on Alaska about what we were doing just for fun. It was probably about 1963 or 1964.

We flew across Cook Inlet from Anchorage and put the plane down. We were roped up on some of the mountains. Some of the guys had climbed Mount McKinley. The rest of us were just eager climbers. In several areas it was safer to be on skis than on foot because of snowed-over crevasses. We were carrying packs of at least fifty-five pounds too. We built snow huts we stayed in. They weren't mobile like tents, but you felt more secure from the wind and cold in a snow hut.

One time as we skied along, Rod fell into a crevasse. That was a close call. Luckily he was on a rope or we might have lost him. It's the crevasses you don't see that will get you. Crevasses are a hazard of Alaska cross-country skiing in the back country. A lot of it was flat ground and that's where skis really come in handy. It's certainly worth packing them up with you. Some of these spots nobody had ever been before.

Quite often our downhill skiing excursions took place outside of Alaska over Christmas when we were visiting family. My father liked to rendezvous at ski resorts over the holidays and Christmas of 1978 we were in Aspen. At that point my mother, Fran, had died and my father had remarried. His second wife was named Marianna.

Getting from Denver to Aspen we split up. My father had asked me to drive the two of them, him and his wife. Tay stayed behind at the Denver airport with a rental car waiting for Dave to fly in and join her. This would have been fine, but we neglected to tell Tay our destination in Aspen. This was in the days before cell phones so we had no way to get in touch with her. At the end of her four-hour drive, Tay had to enlist the help of the local police to find out where L.T. had booked all of us. That upset her no end. Instead of an inn or at the Hotel Jerome, L.T. had rented a private home. I don't think Tay has ever forgotten that one.

For the first few days the temperature in the Rocky Mountains was hovering around zero. It was so cold we went cross-country skiing

A family ski trip on the Eagle Glacier.

instead of downhill skiing. A few days later my father and Marianna departed, but Dave, Tay, and I stayed around for some fast skiing before he had to head back to Dartmouth where he was soon to be named captain of the Nordic ski team. Apparently our children inherited the skiing gene. Interest was passed on from L.T. Sr. to me and then to Anne and Dave.

Tay and I stayed behind after everyone else departed. We fell in love with the place and this turned out to be the first of about twelve December–January visits we took there. Snowmass offers about four separate ski areas with everything from green beginner slopes to double black expert slopes, nearly all perfectly groomed.

Skiing really has been a lifelong interest and passion of mine. I enjoyed it from the start and it kept me active for most of my life. Getting older eventually interfered, though. I think I was eighty-eight, about eight decades after I first started downhill skiing, when I gave it up. I didn't go downhill skiing that year for the first time, I guess the winter of 2010–11. Then I didn't even go cross-country skiing in 2012.

Even in later years when we didn't go back to Colorado, I still went to Alyeska. About four or five years ago the altitude started to bother us. That's when we stopped visiting Snowmass. That was some great skiing in those mountains.

We kept up cross-country skiing until recently. Living on the Hillside in Anchorage, we have snow all around us. I was still doing it for the exercise more than anything else and we have such a wonderful trail system right nearby. Just drive down the hill a little ways and take off.

22

Mount McKinley
Flight Adventures

After Lowell Thomas left politics he spent even more time flying around Alaska. Much of that was due to the creation of his business Talkeetna Air Taxi. Talkeetna is the small Alaska community located about 115 road miles from Anchorage off the Parks Highway that is known internationally as the jumping-off point for flights to Mount McKinley.

As the highest mountain in North America, Mount McKinley attracts mountaineers from all over the world, as well as intrepid Alaskans who have stared at its perpetually snow-covered slopes for years from afar. At 20,320 feet, McKinley is a mountain that stands alone against the horizon in the Alaska Range. Located between Anchorage and Fairbanks, it is highly visible from each of Alaska's two largest cities on clear days. However, McKinley creates its own weather pattern and can sometimes be shrouded in clouds for days at a time.

The mountain was named after President William McKinley of Ohio, but the common Alaska name for it is Denali, as native people call it. Decades before Alaska became a state, explorers of the Arctic became preoccupied with seeking to reach the summit.

After several attempts by various climbers, the mountain was first scaled by a party led by Hudson Stuck, the archdeacon of the

Yukon. Stuck's expedition reached the summit on June 7, 1913, and the group included Walter Harper, Robert Tatum, and Harry Karstens.

In later decades, Lowell's old friend Bradford Washburn became the first to climb McKinley three times and he also pioneered the West Buttress route on the mountain that became the most popular access to the summit. When climbers began hiring guides to ascend McKinley most of them started from the 7,200-foot Kahiltna Glacier, the route Washburn proved was the easiest. Bush pilots, like Lowell Thomas, ferry climbers and their supplies to the glacier for their attempts at the top and pick them up to take them off the mountain from that glacier when they finish.

In between flying mountaineers seeking to climb McKinley to base camp, Thomas and other flyers carried tourists on sightseeing trips to the peak. From April to June, however, the primary business for some years was hauling mountaineers and their stuff to McKinley.

❖ ❖ ❖

LOWELL: The first guide to make an impact on Mount McKinley was Ray Genet. Genet was from Switzerland and he was an outsized personality who adopted a phrase to inspire his clients. He would shout, "To the summit!" That was his motto. In the spring of 1979, Ray telephoned me and said he would like me to do a little bit of flying for him. He knew I had the Helio Courier with its wheels-skis setup perfect for landing on glaciers.

"Thomas," he said, "I need some help with the flying. These guys here like to work bankers' hours and I often need to move my climbing parties early and late. How about it?"

I jumped at the chance to get more involved in that sort of mountain and glacier flying again. It was just what I needed after all those years in Juneau. That's how I got involved flying to the Kahiltna Glacier. It was perfect weather for my intro too. I flew three climbers and their gear off, but a young fellow came up to me mad as hell, saying I needed a Federal Aviation Association commercial license. I said I was

Lowell, at left, with some McKinley climbers and his Helio Courier airplane on Eagle Glacier.

just helping an old friend. Eventually I became partners with the young man, Doug Geeting. I made a mental note not to accept any payment for the flight in case the FAA protested my flying. But then, soon I did go into business there.

Although I ended up doing it hundreds of times, flying onto the Kahiltna Glacier always demanded full attention. That was McKinley base camp and you had to land on an uphill stretch of snow-covered glacier with a grade of between 5 and 10 percent. You always had to land uphill and take off downhill, regardless of wind direction. This upslope landing called for careful monitoring of airspeed on the approach with enough extra for a smooth landing while the plane was still in a slight climb. That was no problem for me. However, swinging around 180 degrees at the end of the landing, and against the grade, to place the plane in position for taking off was another matter. To make that turnaround even more of a challenge was the condition of the snow, deep and soft, or hard and icy. And then whatever wind was blowing was a factor. Even the best of us failed with this maneuver from time to time. If the plane ended up partially turned, it took three or four strong climbers tugging a rope tied to the tail wheel strut to bring the plane around.

That began what also became fifteen years of flying adventures in Alaska's towering snowy mountains. Later that summer my son, Dave, who had just graduated from Dartmouth, signed on as an assistant guide for Genet in order to get the thousand-dollar climbing fee waived. Genet worked him hard hauling gear and setting up tents, but he reached the summit with most of the party.

The usual time for a climb of Mount McKinley with a guide is about three weeks along the West Buttress route. There is a lot of relaying of equipment and careful traversing of the glacier to avoid crevasse danger. It also takes time to acclimate to the altitude as you go. It is about twelve miles to the fourteen-thousand-foot level. Roping up is critical for safety. Above the fourteen-thousand-foot mark the climb becomes much more serious. Weather, storms, and high winds powerful enough to knock one off his feet halt parties for days in tents. Often someone will fall ill, sometimes requiring a rescue. If someone is struck with pulmonary edema they must be rushed to a lower altitude or the illness can become fatal. Over the years I participated in a number of rescues, many of them as high as fourteen thousand feet. I believe I made a record of thirteen flights with a fixed-wing aircraft to that ledge.

I learned a lot that first season on McKinley, but it was my only season working with Ray Genet. Later that year, on his quest to fulfill a dream and climb Mount Everest, he died on the descent. After working for gas money as a favor for Genet that year I did obtain a commercial pilot's license and pass an FAA exam and spent fourteen more years ferrying climbers to the mountain. I was a commercial pilot, and I could fly people anywhere, but I was just doing it on the side. Then I started doing it as a business.

Genet's companion, Kathy Sullivan kept the climbing business going and my first group in the spring of 1980 was from Germany. It was a party of eighteen and I made seven flights from Talkeetna to the glacier in one day. I never made that many flights in one day again. I had no headquarters in Talkeetna at the time. I used Kathy's home. She hired Mike Covington from Colorado, an experienced Himalayan climber, as the chief guide.

When Tay and I were flying overseas in the midfifties the passenger side still had a control wheel. Flying the Helio Courier back and forth to McKinley I decided to have it removed to eliminate any fear of a panicky rider grabbing the controls. That had finally happened to me a couple of years earlier. We were flying along in moderate turbulence and the person in the seat next to me who had never flown a plane got scared and he only let go of the wheel after I shouted that if he didn't he could kill us all.

In those days the base camp manager was a cheery woman named Frances Randall, a musician from Fairbanks and the member of the Fairbanks Symphony Orchestra who used her spare time on the glacier to practice her violin. Frances was personally concerned for the safety and welfare of every climber. She earned the nickname "Mother Frances."

During the climbing season the Kahiltna Glacier can become a Tower of Babel, with climbers from the United States, Japan, Germany, South Korea, France, Italy, Mexico, and Russia, among others, all present at the same time. The base camp manager has to communicate with all of them, sometimes mediating disputes over tent sites and sometimes sending messages out on their behalf. There were sometimes disputes over flying priorities too. Another veteran pilot, Cliff Hudson, once said, "They can't wait to be flown up and they can't wait to be flown back down."

In 1981 I took over Talkeetna Air Taxi as the majority owner with Doug Geeting as the minority owner. At the time there were three air companies and we all got along well. If there was too much business for one company we passed it on to the other. Much later there were many more companies operating, but as time went on there were many more people signing up to try to climb McKinley too.

In recent years more than a thousand people a season have made the try for the summit, and several times even more. In 1981 there were six hundred climbers.

There were quite a few foreign climbers. They had heard about McKinley for a long time and they were attracted to it because it was the tallest peak in North America. They seemed to have a pretty good respect for the mountain, but they probably didn't understand how severe the weather could be. I think that was always a great surprise because it could get down to subzero weather even in the summer. Very high winds have caused a lot of grief for climbers. I hardly ever heard the details of their trips because it was so noisy in the plane on the flight back to Talkeetna. Then they didn't want to linger when they were down.

Most years I felt we were lucky to break even. My biggest cost was liability insurance, at the time more than thirty years ago, roughly twenty thousand dollars a year. Gas was two dollars a gallon at the time. The going rate for pilots was thirty dollars an hour, but I paid my two pilots forty dollars an hour. We charged climbers 220 dollars for a round-trip ride to the Kahiltna Glacier. Flightseers, a minimum of three at a time, were charged sixty-five dollars.

A never-ending problem was the weather on the mountain, especially at base camp. Sometimes we could reach base camp on a CB radio, but oftentimes not. A few years later it was possible to install a phone at base camp that worked via a twelve-volt battery. I never could figure out how the signal got through to Talkeetna with the other mountains in the way, but it was an improvement.

Over the years, especially in the nineties and into the 2000s, the number of climbers increased. Almost always the success rate was about 50 percent. By the early 2000s about one hundred people had died trying to climb the mountain and it was not always possible to retrieve their bodies. About 50 of them were entombed in the ice.

Bradford Washburn's pioneering of the West Buttress from the south side in the summer of 1951, coupled with the use of the airplane, opened the door for more climbers, reducing expedition time from several months to several weeks. The increased human traffic required National Park Service managers to take on more work. They began charging fees to cover the costs of informational sessions stressing the danger and the hazards. Since my time when I flew the Helio Courier to as high as 14,200 feet, there has been a high altitude rescue at 19,000 feet with a helicopter that went far above my capabilities.

I obtained a second Cessna, but one time, Don, one of my pilots, crashed while trying to take off from a short, frozen lake with two bear hunters and their gear. No one was hurt, even though the hunters weren't wearing their seat belts, but the plane was badly bent and it had to be brought out by helicopter at considerable expense. The FAA suspended our certificate for sixty days because of the seat-belt violation. I wasn't too hard on Don, figuring he had learned an important lesson. Then he did it again the following summer; this time on floats trying to lift off a small lake in the Talkeetna Mountains with a couple of hunters. He ran into rocks, badly damaging the floats, but fortunately not the plane itself. Once again I had to pay for the helicopter.

Tony, another pilot, had one major misadventure with Talkeetna Air Taxi. He flew to Mount Spurr to pick up three climbers, but he got stuck. Worried wives dispatched a helicopter to pick up their men, but Tony stayed there for several days and nights with a minimum of food and water and little emergency gear until I managed to fly him out when the surface snow conditions improved.

A few years earlier I had been stuck in the same place when I flew in to get some climbers. I spent a night in the back of the Helio while the wind blew and the plane rocked. I landed at about five thousand feet, but was unaware it had been raining there for several days, turning the snow into something like wet cement. The snow was such that the plane wouldn't move even with one passenger on board. The climbers' small tent didn't have room for a fourth occupant. The next morning, the four of us, the climbers on snowshoes, and me on skis, tramped down the snow ahead of the plane.

Only one other time did I have to camp out in the plane on a glacier. I was on a pickup of three climbers at the foot of Mount

Hayes, a fourteen-thousand-foot mountain near the eastern end of the Alaska Range. I knew the weather was questionable when I left Talkeetna and the direct route was a no-go. The weather was deteriorating, but when I got there the climbers had marked the landing area with packs and plastic sleds and were standing by their green tent waving.

So land I did. There was no problem until the plane slowed to a stop. That's when the tail ski broke through a heavy crust. The four of us got the plane turned around OK, but not knowing if anyone would come that afternoon they hadn't dismantled their camp and packed. In the next half hour the overcast lowered and it began to snow lightly. I got them into the plane with their stuff and gave her full throttle, but we didn't budge. We tramped down the crusted snow in front of the plane, but it was too late. The layer of dark clouds dropped right onto the glacier and we had zero visibility with heavier, wet snowfall. I was able to get word to Tay about what happened through the radio to a helicopter, and then to the FAA, and spent another uncomfortable, nearly sleepless night in the back of the plane.

I considered supporting climbers in remote regions where no other planes operated as the most challenging, dangerous, and adventuresome of flights. The first danger was unknown glacier conditions because there could be snow-covered crevasses. Retrieving climbers was the most worrisome task because of their dependence on the plane. After a number of years I finally gave up flying climbers into total wilderness. At least Mount McKinley had an organized base camp.

Talkeetna Air Taxi also served the general public. That meant flying miners, hunters, trappers, and flightseers. By the mid-1990s flightseeing had become the main business. One time I flew a few geologists to the Taylor Mountains several hundred miles southwest of Anchorage. The job entailed shuttling them around to several locations, none of which had a landing field or human habitation. The chief geologist arranged for fuel drums to be dropped off in advance, but I had to refuel with a hand pump. One takeoff near the end of the job was close to becoming a disaster. We took off from a snow-covered swamp with a number of stunted spruce I had to dodge. That isn't an easy task when the plane is on skis and brakes are useless.

The snow had softened since I made another takeoff from the same spot and I barely got the plane airborne to clear a stand of trees at the end of the swamp. The skis might even have brushed a few top limbs. I should have stopped the run as soon as I noticed our slow acceleration and taxied the plane several times over snow to pack it down before another attempt.

Those who fly McKinley and its neighbors are no strangers to tragedy among climbers. I flew out three who perished during the eighties. My first retrieval came at the request of Ranger Roger Robinson. A Japanese climber had died of pulmonary edema early in his party's ascent, surprisingly only at about ten thousand feet. The body had been lowered to base camp. It was hard to understand how this death occurred at that altitude. Usually well-conditioned climbers aren't affected by altitude until they get up higher. You don't really look forward to that kind of flight, but it has to be done. You've got to get them off the mountain if you can.

The other unfortunates I brought down were picked up at the 14,200 level. One was a Polish climber, the other a German. Both were victims of falls, perhaps trying to take a shortcut to the fourteen-thousand-foot-high camp. A spot on McKinley has rather ghoulishly been named "The Orient Express" because so many Japanese and Korean climbers came to disaster at the extremely steep, rock-studded gully.

Except for body retrievals, I enjoyed and was proud of my flights to that height on the mountain. Yes, my plane had a turbo charger that enabled it to fly higher than others, but I also believe my skill and good judgment played a part in allowing me to land at fourteen thousand feet thirteen times with a fixed-wing aircraft. First, I had to put myself on oxygen after climbing above ten thousand feet. After that I climbed to fifteen thousand feet for a very careful circle over the shelf while checking for downdrafts. Any turbulence would rule out a landing. While circling I made sure the landing area was marked. The approach was spectacular over the glacier.

When it was time to depart, I always had to worry about restarting the engine. At that altitude I had to tease the mixture control and the engine wouldn't accept the full, rich mixture until nearly revved to full power. Since my time the Park Service has refused to allow planes to land there, only helicopters.

One time with two German climbers aboard who had suffered frozen feet, the engine did fail. I had to make a forced landing on a private gravel strip a few miles north of Willow, on the Rustic Wilderness airstrip. A red light came on announcing low turbo oil pressure. Quick as I could I pulled back the throttle, cut the mixture, put the prop in coarse pitch, and pulled the nose up close to a stall. That stopped the propeller. I knew I could glide to the Parks Highway or to a sandbar on the Susitna River, but neither option seemed appealing.

Another time, accompanied by Chief Ranger Bob Seibert, I flew up high on McKinley to drop an oxygen bottle for a rescue in progress. Others were trying to save a climber suffering from pulmonary edema. Bob and I put on oxygen masks and flew up to about nineteen thousand feet. I was glad to find the upper air calm with no signs of downdrafts. Bob could not spot the rescue party, but guided me to a spot where he could drop the bottle on the usual trail in the hopes they would find it.

In 1981, I was invited to begin flying for Wally Cole, the owner of Camp Denali at Wonder Lake, using the airstrip at Kantishna. That wonderful relationship lasted till 1994. I brought the guests to the remote lodge. Then I provided flightseeing trips around McKinley for those who wanted to go. For a time that was my primary business.

The end of the 1981 climbing season brought the news of my father's death. L.T. was still active to the end, and he was nearly ninety years old. He passed away in his own bed at Quaker Hill in Pawling, New York. I was distressed not to have been with him at the end. I hurried back east for services. When I returned to Alaska, Tay and I visited Wally Cole and his wife, Jerrie, who were closing up the lodge for the season. We got stuck there for a week because of the weather and played a lot of Monopoly. It proved to be a good retreat to get over the

A view of Mount McKinley's Kahiltna Glacier in 1981 after Lowell learned his father Lowell Sr. had passed away.

shock and sadness of losing such a wonderful parent. Over the years, with all of the time I spent there, Camp Denali became like a second home. This was especially true over a couple of summers when Tay traveled to Switzerland and another time to the Holy Land.

Still, throughout the eighties the main task was ferrying mountain climbers from Talkeetna to Mount McKinley and back. The climbers came from everywhere. I flew Germans, Swiss, Italians, even a team from Taiwan. I got some excellent film footage of the mountains, the climbers, and once, of a rescue when I flew top cover [above the clouds] reporting to the helicopter about the wind conditions. Quite a few of the mountaineers had already climbed in the Himalayas and the Andes. A large percentage of climbers came from the lower states. One I'll long remember came from Arizona and was not experienced with snow and ice mountains. He showed up wearing light hiking boots. I assumed his heavy boots were in a duffle, but at base camp Frances put him under house arrest.

There was one chap from Romania who showed up several different seasons saying he was going to try McKinley by himself. But he always tried to attach himself to another party and sought to sponge their food and fuel. The pilots, the guides, and rangers got to cringing when he showed up. A freeloader who looks to others for his care and protection has no business on the mountain. All of the others seemed to be first-rate men and women ready and able to carry their loads and bear responsibility for their actions.

It was the Russians I enjoyed the most. About a dozen came over each year in an exchange with the American Alpine Club and I flew them for free. Several brought along guitars and we had some grand evenings of Russian songs and much laughter while they waited several days at the Talkeetna Inn for suitable flying weather.

There were others who sought to make solo climbs of Denali. One year, on August 1, very late in the season, I flew an Italian woman named Marie Ercolani off the mountain. When I picked her up she said she had made it to the summit alone—that would have been the first solo ascent by a woman. Barbara Washburn had made the first ascent by a woman with Brad in 1947. Ercolani could offer no proof, such as a summit photo, and there was only one other person left on the mountain. A few of us doubt that she made it to the top.

However, Norma Jean Saunders, an Alaska guide and experienced McKinley climber, was a woman who definitely made it on her own to the summit in June of 1990, taking twelve days from Kahiltna base camp. She waited on the summit until others arrived to witness her presence there.

By far the most memorable soloist at the time was Japanese adventurer Naomi Uemura, a world-class adventurer who had already made a solo climb of McKinley in 1970, driven a dog team across the Greenland icecap, and was the first from his country to climb Mount Everest. When he showed up in Alaska in February of 1984 his plan was to make the first winter solo of McKinley. He was accompanied by a Japanese camera crew. For some reason I was away when the day came to fly Uemura to the mountain and Doug Geeting flew him.

The rescue of a Japanese mountaineer on Mount McKinley.

As protection against climbing alone in a crevasse area, Uemura rigged up a fifteen-foot bamboo pole that he hoped would help him if he fell. He wore a bright, red climbing suit and that made him easy to spot from the air. When I returned I flew the cameraman around for shots of Uemura in midclimb. Uemura was living on raw caribou meat and one day we dropped him a package of sushi while he was at fourteen thousand feet.

After seeing Uemura at that elevation the weather moved in and blocked out the mountain so we lost track of his progress. Then on a Sunday afternoon, February 12, I took two cameramen to the mountain hoping to spot Uemura. Solid clouds obscured everything as we searched. Suddenly, there was break in the clouds and my passengers spotted the red suit. We heard his voice on the CB radio. He was nearing Denali Pass, which was at 17,200 feet and was going for the summit. He said he had been storm-bound in an ice cave at 17,000 feet for several days. Our glimpse of Uemura and the brief radio contact were the last ever.

Mount McKinley with the Muldrow Glacier and Harper Icefall visible.

Later, Uemura's caribou skin blanket and sleeping bag were found in the cave which must have been his final camp. He was never seen again and no trace of his body was ever found. Doug Geeting and I spent hours spread out over several days searching the West Buttress and higher up. A national hero in Japan, there was great mourning over Uemura in his home country.

On February 22, I went up alone to have a look along the north side of the peak, the upper Harper Glacier, in case Naomi had been blown over that way. I climbed to a bit more than twenty thousand feet, proceeding from west to east in smooth air. Abruptly, the bottom fell out. Plane and I went into a freefall. Stuff in the back that wasn't tied down went floating in the air. I hit my head on the ceiling despite my tight seat belt. Papers and pencils went soaring. Never have I experienced such a downdraft. The engine continued to run while I wrestled with the controls to keep us right-side up. In less than thirty seconds I dropped six thousand feet to fourteen thousand feet. That was an incredible rate of descent. It was an aerial Niagara Falls.

How lucky for me that the plane's momentum carried me away from McKinley's face.

Naomi Uemura's fate will forever be a mystery. Many members of the Japanese press sought me out in Alaska. Naomi's diary was found at his fourteen-thousand-foot base camp and it contained a possible clue about what happened—he said he was having trouble keeping his crampons fastened to his large rubber Bunny Boots. It is possible that a crampon may have come off, sending him into a fatal slide into a crevasse. Or he may have wandered off a ledge in whiteout conditions, or simply become exhausted.

Then his widow came over from Japan and I took her flying to the mountain so she could pay her last respects to him.

One thing we do know for sure is that Naomi Uemura reached the summit. The team of Japanese climbers who visited McKinley found a Japanese flag tied to a metal rod at the summit, tied with what they said was a strip of his underwear. Uemura achieved the goal of being the first to reach the summit of Mount McKinley alone in winter, but he did not complete his solo by returning safely to sea level to tell about it.

Mount McKinley is spellbinding. I always liked to look at it. I even look out the window every day at home trying to see it.

23

Flying Another
McKinley Soloist

In February of 1988, four years after Naomi Uemura sought to become the first mountain climber to make a solo winter ascent of 20,320-foot Mount McKinley, another climber, this time an Alaskan named Vernon Tejas, came to Lowell Thomas Jr. with the same idea.

Tejas, who was a guide on Mount McKinley, had been to the summit several times already while leading citizen climbers, wished to try to do what Uemura did, but make it successfully back to Talkeetna and Anchorage. Firmly built, though not very tall, Tejas owned a thick, black beard that was complemented by a shaven head. He was known for playing songs on his harmonica to entertain his climbing clients in their camps.

Having been on McKinley's slopes many times during the spring climbing season and witnessed the peak throwing temper tantrums of high winds and daunting blizzards at climbers, Tejas had no illusions that making a winter climb would be easy. He chose to depart in mid-February, with the idea that the ascent might well carry over into March, which might be helpful, not because warmer weather was expected, but because there would be more hours of daylight to use to his advantage than there would be in December or January.

Well aware of the danger posed by crevasses and how easy it would be for him to fall into a deep chasm and never be heard from again, Tejas, like Uemura, rigged up a special protective device that presumably would catch him if he took a tumble. While Uemura invented his bamboo waist-line gizmo, Tejas fashioned a similar-style item out of an aluminum ladder.

If any more knowledge of the likelihood of extreme weather and danger was needed beyond Tejas's own experience on the mountain, all he had to do was look at the example of Uemura, a world-class adventurer with loads of cold-weather and mountaineering experience who died trying to make the summit. Tejas did not want to die, but he did want to reach the summit, and he sought Lowell Thomas Jr.'s expertise to fly him to the Kahiltna Glacier.

❖ ❖ ❖

LOWELL: The challenge of a first successful solo winter climb of North America's tallest mountain was too much for one of Alaska's climbers to ignore. Vern Tejas, a McKinley guide famous for his rescues and for climbs in the Andes and Himalayas, decided to give it a try.

I was delighted to fly him to the Kahiltna Glacier on February 16, 1988, using the Helio. His twelve-foot aluminum ladder, however, posed a problem. It was too long to fit into the cabin. To get it into the plane I had to take down the panel at the back of the cabin so that the last foot of the ladder could extend into the rear of the fuselage. At the same time its front end rested on the instrument panel. Vern and I had to lean slightly to each side of the cockpit with the ladder between us.

It was a fine morning for approaching McKinley. No other planes were in the air as we neared the glacier's southeast fork. There was not a trace of the previous year's base camp, nor any tracks in the snow. Snowfall at that seven-thousand-foot level had probably totaled ten feet or more since the end of the last climbing season, wiping out any indication people had ever been there. It was totally back to nature. I lingered on the glacier just long enough to help unload and note that Vern cached some food items off to one side, marking the spot with a tall wand.

A few weeks passed and I went searching for the soloist, listening on my CB radio for his voice. No sighting, no contact. I went up again on March 8 and this time I was able to talk with him, though I didn't fly high enough to see him. I told him I had landed an hour earlier, but could not find his cache, so unloaded some new boxes of dried food and some fuel just in case he needed them at the end of the trip.

Vern did not say anything about reaching the summit, but he must have told me he was about to start down. Some bad weather roared in and I did not return for six days. There he was, waiting for a ride home. In between, however, there had been great worry about Vern's fate on the mountain. It had only been a few years since Uemura disappeared and there had been no contact with Vern after I reported seeing him a week earlier. Many wondered if he was dead or alive. Prayers were being said for Vern. The silence was very loud.

Yes, Vern did reach the summit. He also had some serious difficulties. The wicked weather had trapped Vern in a snow cave for some days at around seventeen thousand feet of altitude while he waited out the storm. Vern said he thought about Naomi many times during the twenty-eight days he was on the mountain and that once while reclining in the snow cave he felt a breeze. He said he spoke aloud, "Good morning" to the Japanese adventurer. Vern also said, "I felt his spirit up there."

Vern's solo had a happy ending. He safely returned from Mount McKinley and he caused a bit of a sensation. He gained a considerable amount of fame and collaborated on a book about his adventure. After that Vern was not only quite renowned, but kept adding to his accomplishments with many other adventures. He became the first mountaineer to complete a solo ascent of Mount Vinson, the tallest peak in Antarctica, and he completed the Seven Summits challenge, climbing the tallest mountains on each of the seven continents. And although twenty-five years have passed, Vern continues to guide on Mount McKinley each season, having made more than fifty ascents to the summit.

I can tell you as a pilot it is much more pleasant to fly a mountaineer to his destination who achieves something great, and then returns alive to talk about it rather than having to search the mountain for a body.

In 1988, Lowell flew Alaskan mountain climber Vern Tejas to 20,320-foot Mount McKinley—and back—as Tejas completed his historic first solo winter ascent of the tallest peak in North America.

The saga of Mount McKinley climbs and tragedies continues every year. Every single person who attempts to climb that challenging mountain is embarking on his or her own adventure, whether it is any kind of first or not. Anyone who successfully negotiates the climb and returns home safely has accomplished something special.

While we are unlikely ever to determine what happened to Naomi Uemura and unlikely ever to discover his body, unusual things do occur. Several years ago some determined climbers searched and found the body of George Mallory, who was lost on Mount Everest in 1924. In 2004, some climbers came across the body of a climber who died on McKinley thirty-five years earlier. They found the body around the seventeen-thousand-foot mark on the West Buttress. Melting in the area or the wind exposed it over time. The Park Service investigation uncovered the man's identity—he had been on a 1969 climb. From others in his party it was learned that he had fallen sick with what we now know was pulmonary edema. As he weakened, and apparently without realizing the seriousness of his condition, the other members of his party left him behind and went on to the summit. Upon their return the man was in desperate condition and he soon passed away.

Unable to carry the man back down the mountain they yielded to his last wish—that his body be left on Mount McKinley. Rather remarkably, the rangers were able to reach this man's widow and she asked that he be reburied on the mountain. Mount McKinley only reluctantly gives up its secrets.

No matter how well-prepared one is for flying in the mountains and landing on glaciers in Alaska, surprises happen like the downdraft that struck my plane when I was searching for Uemura. In July of 1987 I was carrying four sightseers to the Ruth Glacier and just at the moment of touchdown the right ski tore off, forcing the plane to swerve sharply to the right and come to a sudden stop. Thank the Lord it did not nose over. This was a first and another pilot had to come in to haul out the passengers and drop off a mechanic. The problem was diagnosed as equipment failure, but the mechanic had to return to Talkeetna and left me behind with the plane.

I tried a few maneuvers to produce a takeoff, but the wheels just dug deeper in the snow. I grabbed my sleeping bag and skied a few hundred yards to the Don Sheldon Mountain House intending to stay the night, but my mind wouldn't rest as I sought a solution. An improvisational idea came to me. If I let the air out of the tire on the damaged right side, so that the ski was in its up position and met the snow, and pumped the left ski into the down position it would make the plane tilt to starboard, but the drag of the right wheel might be eliminated. If this worked, the landing back in Talkeetna would have to be with the skis down. But so what? That wouldn't do anything more than scratch their bottoms. That plan worked and I took off. About twenty miles out from Talkeetna I informed the air traffic controller that I was going to land on the gravel at my office instead of the paved runway. The plane and I landed OK. I was fortunate that I never had a ski failure in a completely remote location, though I guess some people would consider the Ruth Glacier to be remote.

Once, I had a call from the National Outdoor Leadership School asking if I could fly some food and fuel onto the Science Glacier in the Chugach Mountain Range for a party of a dozen or so guided students. It entailed flying to Palmer in the Matanuska-Susitna Valley first for eight hundred pounds of supplies to be loaded. I flew up the Knik Glacier by Mount Marcus Baker and landed at the eight-thousand-foot level of the glacier. To say this is a spectacular region of mountains and glaciers is a huge understatement. What appealed to me was being alone on this flight facing the challenge of an extremely remote landing on a glacier never touched before by a plane. I set down in the shade of a mountain.

I was days ahead of the NOLS party, so I didn't want to get stuck in the snow. I suppose I could have lived on their supplies while I waited for them. I placed my freight in a pile and marked it with an eight-foot wand. After taking care of that I put my skis on and went touring up the glacier to a point where I could look down onto College Fjord. What a sight from nine thousand feet!

Later, in August of 1999, I joined National Park Rangers Daryl Miller and Ralph Tingey and Alaskan climber Charles Sassara on a mission to conduct an independent investigation of the disappearance of a young male NOLS student on the Matanuska Glacier a month or so earlier near the end of a guided expedition. The purpose of the trip was to train students in glacier travel and snow and ice climbing. At the end of the trip NOLS students are left alone and unsupervised to put into practice what they learned. The missing lad had last been seen searching to fill two pots of water for dinner with his campmates.

I flew the group to an airstrip near Sheep Mountain, but we had to transfer to a smaller Super Cub after that. I was the first one dropped off and had time to think. Something on this river of ice had snatched a young fellow. We had a strenuous hike to the last camp and noted there were a number of trickles and streams of meltwater flowing by. We walked down the slippery sloping ice carefully for a close look. We could hear sounds like a waterfall a little way down-glacier. It turned out to be coming from a "moulin," which is defined as "a near vertical shaft in a glacier caused by meltwater." The hole was large enough to swallow a person. Had the student slipped on the sloping ice bank it would have been extremely difficult to avoid falling into the stream and being swept into the hole. That's what we decided most likely had happened. What a grim way to leave this world.

Probably my two most famous passengers were Charles Lindbergh, who didn't trust the plane without inspecting it, and newsman Walter Cronkite, who was addressing a graduating class at the University of Alaska, I believe. His wife did not want to join us on the flight on a gorgeous afternoon. As soon as we set down on the Kahiltna Glacier, an avalanche roared down the east face of Mount Foraker. "Quite a show!" he said.

A number of climbers were either just starting out from base camp or were just retreating from the summit and they thought they got quite a show too, because they had looks of amazement on their faces when they recognized Walter Cronkite. Many pictures were snapped and hands shaken and Walter asked them about their experiences on the mountain. Frances Randall invited him into her tent for a cup of tea. A few years later while reading the Cronkite biography I was pleased to see that he mentioned our flight together.

Of course, he stated that the pilot was the son of his longtime friend Lowell Thomas Sr. But he wrote that my airplane was a slow, rickety machine held together with bailing wire and chewing gum. Which it was not and is not! That aspersion I did not appreciate. It was surprising he did not show a better understanding of light aircraft and the importance of using slow-flying planes in this sort of work.

I've had others question my plane—like a family from out of state that I flew from Anchorage to Camp Denali. I wondered why they were so quiet as we flew over the swamps and tundra of the Susitna Valley and then over the forty miles of the Kahiltna Glacier and on to Wonder Lake. Upon landing at the end of the gorgeous flight the wife said had she known we would be in such a small plane she wouldn't have agreed to it. I guess the reaction should be no surprise coming from people who have never flown in anything smaller than a Boeing 737.

Then there was the male guest from Camp Denali who pretty much panicked ten minutes out of Kantishna as we neared the Muldrow Glacier. He broke out in a sweat and began to shake. My only option was to turn around and cancel the flight. I wondered why he got on in the first place. Another time, I took out a lady on a McKinley flight who should have known better. After it was over her friend told me she had heart trouble and was supposed to stay at low altitudes. I had taken her to twelve thousand feet. One of my passengers (not this one) died at the camp. Walking up to his cabin at breakfast time he fell over by the side of the trail, dead when found. Heart medicine was discovered amongst his things in the cabin.

Throughout most of the eighties I flew climbers to McKinley. Gradually, through 1994, my focus turned more to tourists at Camp Denali. I always enjoyed showing visitors the gorgeous scenery of Alaska and hoped they appreciated what they were seeing. For that purpose I acquired a larger plane, a seven-seat Cessna 207. What a performer! Managing a wonderful new turbine engine was the main thing to be learned for me. The constant eighteen hundred prop rpm for all phases of flight was a surprise. That made for a quieter and smoother flight. However, fuel consumption was greater.

To keep weight and balance within limits I would put the heaviest person next to me in the right seat, the next two heaviest right behind me, and two more in the next rear seat, with the lightest person in the aft seat. Occasionally I got it wrong and the plane would tell me by squatting its tail on the ground. Very embarrassing. This was particularly the case in Allakaket where I'd gone to fly native women to an Episcopal gathering in Fairbanks. The plane sat down as the last Eskimo woman climbed into the rear seat. Even when I told her that readjusting the load would correct the situation she opted to stay behind. No one could change her mind.

On scenic flights in the 207 from Kantishna, my usual route was over the McKinley bar to McGonagall Pass, across the Muldrow Glacier, climbing up the Traleika Glacier and over the pass to the Sheldon Amphitheatre, circling for good views out each side, all the while giving the passengers a running commentary over the PA system. I'd tell about the Sourdoughs from Fairbanks attempting to make the first ascent of McKinley in 1910, the Harper Icefall, and Hudson Stuck's first ascent via Karsten's Ridge, and the naming of the Amphitheatre for legendary pilot Don Sheldon, who died of cancer in 1975. All the while I pretty much kept the plane at eleven thousand feet. The whole trip took about an hour and some days I made as many as three or four trips by midafternoon.

Wally and Jerrie Cole used to throw an end-of-season party after the last guests departed from Camp Denali and I always tried to make it from Anchorage. One time there was cloud buildup and I had to fly up to eighteen thousand feet near McKinley while wearing oxygen. I was determined to make the party because I was bringing six gallons of ice cream in a cooler. At high altitude, with a reduction in atmospheric pressure, the ice cream was affected in a strange way. It expanded, pushing up the lids of each half-gallon carton several inches. At dessert time Wally showed the cartons to everybody and said, "Look what happens to ice cream at eighteen thousand feet." But it tasted as good as ever.

My fifteen years of commercial flying to mountains and glaciers, throughout the Alaska Range and onto Mount McKinley, produced some of the most rewarding experiences of my life. My first encounter with North America's tallest mountain came while producing a television film about our new state during the summer of 1958. As I looked at the mountain for the first time with its four-mile-high mass of sparkling snow and ice it beckoned to me like the flame of a candle beckons a moth.

The challenge was always to cope with Denali's fickle nature, to read its moods and to know when a flight would or would not succeed. Along with poor visibility, when clouds, snow, and fog hung about, the greatest threat I faced was from downdrafts strong enough to toss a plane thousands of feet up and down. Only experience taught me how to read nature's warning signs.

Dangerous living, for sure, but the very danger of mountain flying is a large part of the appeal. It's the challenge along with the fun and adventure—and the wild, scenic beauty.

24

To Russia with Love

The great thaw in the cold war began in the late 1980s when Mikhail Gorbachev became the Soviet Union's new chief of state. People in the West became familiar with Russian terms like *glasnost* and *perestroika*, or openness and restructuring. Then, in 1989, the Berlin Wall, the most odious symbol of separateness between the USSR and the rest of Europe, came down.

While like most Americans Alaskans cheered this sign of détente the outlook was different. At its closest spot, Alaska is two and a half miles from the Russian border. Facing one another across the Bering Strait are inhabitants or visitors to Big Diomede Island belonging to Russia, and Little Diomede Island, part of Alaska.

Alaska, the territory that once belonged to Russia, and the Soviet Far East, felt a kinship. The Native peoples of both islands and the mainland in those areas were in some cases relatives that had not seen one another for decades.

A movement grew to improve ties between the two large landmasses that some thought might have more in common with each other than with their own capitals of government thousands of miles away in Moscow or Washington, D.C. Regional leaders reached out to one another and friendship forays were organized. Alaska Airlines took some baby steps toward regular passenger service between Alaska and selected cities of the Soviet Far East. A new dog-sled race, entitled the Hope race, was instituted, and Alaskan dog mushers participated.

Intrigued by these happenings, Lowell Thomas Jr., who had always had an interest in visiting previously closed-to-tourists foreign lands, got into the mix through a June 1990 flight to one more formerly forbidden land—Siberia.

Thomas was already fifty-seven years old when he bought the majority interest in Talkeetna Air Taxi and he sold the business in 1994 when he was seventy. But in between he had one refreshing opportunity to fly again to a new place he had only dreamed of visiting by airplane. In the 1950s, Thomas had proposed a flight to the Soviet Union, but had been rebuffed. In the summer of 1990, Thomas was off to the city of Provideniya.

❖ ❖ ❖

LOWELL: "Provideniya Control, this is Cessna 70549, over." My son, David, and I were a bit tense as we attempted our first radio contact with the Russians. We were an hour and a half out of Nome and had crossed most of the Bering Sea at ten thousand feet in my prop-jet Cessna 207. St. Lawrence Island, the last of Alaska, had dropped behind. Soviet airspace was just minutes away and thoughts of Mig fighters came to mind.

"549, Provideniya," came the welcome voice, followed by broken English that we couldn't understand. At least the Soviets knew we were on the way, good to know in case the flight plan filed in Nome had not yet reached them. I answered that we were cruising at three thousand meters and estimated our arrival on the hour.

"549, Provideniya," we heard again with a hard-to-understand request. Dave and I exchanged worried glances. "Didn't I hear the word 'Valta?'" Dave said. That was it. The controller wanted to know where we would penetrate Soviet airspace.

"Provideniya, 549—Larsa, Larsa," I radioed. "Ten minutes to Larsa." That was merely a dot on the map, one of three points of entry

In 1990, Lowell and David were able to fly their own plane from Nome, Alaska, to Provideniya in Siberia, and here Lowell is taking care of the refueling before flying home.

only recently established, one of three cracks in the ice curtain a US plane, with prior clearance, could slip through. I chose Larsa because it offered the least time with over-water flying.

Dave and I were fulfilling a dream that for me went back to the late 1950s when the Russian Embassy in Washington turned down a similar request. There was no glasnost in Nikita Khrushchev's time. Alaska and Russia are so close together in certain places that over my thirty years of flying in Alaska I had once in a while flown within sight of that forbidden land, which might as well have been on another planet.

I was invited on one of the first Alaska Airlines friendship flights in 1988 and then I applied to come with my own plane with my son as navigator. It was a great adventure to fly from Alaska to this place right over here that we could almost see, but where we were never allowed to go. There was a lot of interaction springing up at the time and once even my rotary group went over to Siberia. I just wanted to do it for the sake of going over by airplane. I didn't have another big purpose. It wasn't to stay long, it was just the trip. The idea was to hop over this narrow body of water to our next-door neighbor that for so long had been a forbidden place.

Miraculously, with a changing political climate, the door was ajar. Dave, who is also a pilot, and I, not only had an invitation from past and present mayors of Provideniya, we had passports and visas allowing us entry. In addition, we also had what we later learned was the first Soviet permit for a single-engine private plane out of Alaska. The permit from the Ministry of Civil Aviation of the USSR read, "CLR CFMD TO OPRT THE FLT WITHOUT SOVIET NAVIGATOR IN ACCORDANCE WITH THE REQUEST." Alaskan Jerry Tokar, who was born in the Ukraine, played a large role in improving Alaskan-Soviet relations at the time and his assistance was crucial for us to gain the permit.

Larsa is a point on the US-Russia Convention Line of 1867 that is exactly twenty-four nautical miles from Gambell on St. Lawrence Island and directly on course to a powerful radio beacon known as "Bravo Charlie" at the entrance to Provideniya Bay. As we began our descent, the sea below was calm. Off to our right were treeless, mostly snow-covered hills and rocky cliffs. Then Tkachen Bay opened up, still choked with ice on June 6 on that side of the International Dateline. We turned to the right at a bluff and there was the airport five miles away at the north end of a narrow lake. The town of Provideniya nestled against a barren mountain another few miles beyond. We were right on our estimated time of arrival of 10:00 A.M. local time, a flight of an hour and fifty-seven minutes from Nome.

Stepping onto our neighbors' soil for the first time was an exciting moment for both of us, as was being greeted by an English-speaking official named George Nechaev. Behind him were two uniformed border guards and an unsmiling, all-business Russian wearing a dark suit and tie. He was the customs inspector. We had to show that we had no drugs, no gold, no bank drafts, and nothing for sale. We carefully counted and declared our dollars. We had quite a few of those because we had to pay for aircraft fuel and anything else in US dollars.

We locked down the plane and jumped into a government jeep with George and his driver, Roman Melnechuk. There was nothing somber about them. They were open and friendly.

Provideniya lay at the head of a bay and we made our way there over a bouncy, dirt road best suited for a stout four-by-four vehicle. As we approached the town we saw the typical Russian cement slab buildings three-to-five stories high along the harbor. The colors varied from orange to faded pink to unpainted cement gray. Roman skillfully dodged foot-deep potholes left over from a winter about as severe as Barrow's, but with snowfall equal to that of Valdez. That meant it was very cold and also very snowy, not simply either-or.

Known as "The Gateway to Chukotka," the city of six thousand people at the time had the no-frills feel of a frontier town. Established in 1933, the community was a regional hub for native communities and settlements scattered along the coast and inland.

As a courtesy call we were led to the office of Alexander Batura, the chairman of the region. He welcomed us in Russian, which we didn't understand, and I told him it was a dream come true to fly from nearby Alaska in my own plane.

There were no private homes in Provideniya, only apartment buildings, and our base was to be Roman's fifth-floor, two-room apartment. One room overlooked the harbor where a freighter was at anchor and an icebreaker was moored to a dock. The other room looked out on a rubble-strewn courtyard, other cement buildings, and a barren rock wall. Roman said his wife was in Vladivostok and he put together a meal in his tiny kitchen that consisted of vegetable borscht, peas, and mashed potatoes, and the famous, excellent Russian bread, which is a staple throughout the country, some red wine, and a locally brewed beer.

We took an afternoon stroll and that impressed upon us the austerity in a farthest outback corner of the Russian Republic. Nearly all of the buildings looked the same, no doubt functional, but drab. We saw a school, the hospital, and an indoor Olympic-sized saltwater pool that was used for physical therapy and children's swimming lessons. We never saw more than a few people on the street at one time.

We surmised that there wasn't much to lure them away from their jobs or apartments, with one exception. We came across a several-hundred-gallon tank on wheels dispensing beer. As we walked past, a dozen or so locals were filling glass containers. Beer and bread seemed to be the only items Provideniya's residents found in abundance.

Passing a bank we suggested changing dollars into rubles in order to purchase some small gifts to bring home, but George said it was pointless because the only things worth buying were native ivory or skins and we were prohibited from bringing them into the United States.

Looming over Provideniya was a brick stack about two hundred feet tall that emitted a constant dark plume of smoke from the central coal-burning power plant. We thought that it might be wise to install something that limited the air pollution, but George said most people did not really care. We wondered if the people just came and worked a stint for a few years and then returned to Magadan, Leningrad, or wherever.

In the evening we visited the icebreaker, which had only recently opened up the harbor. It was not nuclear powered, we were told by Valerie, the captain, but it was large, with a crew of sixty-five, including a dozen women. The ship was big enough to have a helicopter parked on the stern which was used to scout ice ahead. Usually based in Vladivostok, the icebreaker's mission was to keep ports and sea lanes opened along the Bering Sea and Arctic Ocean coasts.

The next day we learned that two Alaskans arrived in the wee hours without visas or even passports. An Aeroflot plane returning from Fairbanks following the first reunion of American and Russian World War II land-lease pilots was supposed to drop off two Alaskans in Nome, but due to the weather had not landed and deposited them in Provideniya instead. George had been called in to help resolve the issue of visitors with no papers. Imagine how serious that would have been in the days of Stalin. The two men joined us for breakfast. We would have flown them back with us, but that would have been illegal because we removed the backseats in favor of emergency gear for crossing the Bering Strait. We were told that Nome-based Bering Air was due to fly in the next day anyway with some Alaskans to celebrate Friendship Day.

George called Bering Air's owner Jim Rowe and put me on the phone to explain the situation. We secured a ride for the Alaskans. Rowe and his company deserved considerable credit for opening up the air corridor between Alaska and Provideniya at that time. He started by urging the Soviet Union to allow businesspeople and government people on flights and gradually ordinary people were allowed to travel back and forth.

On our second day Dave and I hiked up a mountain, visited the local museum, and had lunch with our primary sponsor, Oleg Kulinkin, the former mayor. As we climbed the peak we ran across clusters of bright yellow wildflowers in the midst of the rocks, the same as I had seen in northern Alaska. Dave scrambled to the top at about two thousand feet, while I stopped halfway up. My vantage point gave me a sweeping view of Provideniya Bay. The northwest arm was still completely covered in ice.

Although the museum was supposed to be closed for reorganization we talked our way in and were shown ivory carvings, native clothing, and ancient hunting tools. They were similar to those of early Alaska natives. One room featured things brought from Alaska and there was a fine painting by famous Alaskan artist Fred Machetanz.

The lunch plan revolved around meeting Oleg Kulinkin at a different apartment in another five-story building. Jerry Tokar had tipped me off that Kulinkin was a painter in his spare time, but found materials hard to obtain in Provideniya, so we brought a gift of oil paints and paper for charcoal drawings. Kulinkin seemed quite delighted to receive these.

It occurred to me that we never saw any senior citizens in town. Except for that accidental visit by the Alaskan World War II vet, I was probably the oldest fellow in town. We were joined for lunch by Kulinkin's wife, Galena, and Jim Stimpfle from Nome, who had been in town for weeks working on developing outdoor activities such as rafting and fishing trips for American tourists. Jim had been involved in organizing the first Friendship Day delegation from Alaska when Alaska Airlines brought Governor Steve Cowper and US Senator Frank Murkowski to Provideniya. A highlight of that trip was reuniting Alaska Eskimos with relatives on the Soviet side for the first time since the border was closed in 1948.

The menu for our lunch included sausage patties, rice pilaf, cucumbers, bread, and a tasty, warm fruit drink. More Provideniya beer was offered, but because we were going to be flying back later we avoided imbibing. George acted as full-time translator. I conveyed how much it meant to us to be able to make the visit and Galena Kulinkin raved about her visit to Anchorage during the past year, exclaiming over the city's beauty and its greenness, as well as the plenty of goods available in the stores.

Another visitor arrived, a young woman in her twenties named Tanya, who spoke English so well I thought she must have lived and studied in the United States. But she said no, she had learned at the University of Moscow and was in Provideniya to teach English. Conversation shifted to politics and I explained that Americans were impressed by Gorbachev and that we credited him with ending the cold war and liked him because of his charming ways. Tanya said many Russians preferred Boris Yeltsin because they felt he would be a stronger leader. Indeed, Yeltsin did become the next leader, following Gorbachev, and he was called upon to show his strength and resolve at critical times.

As we returned to the airport, Dave and I and Roman and George exchanged gifts. We presented Roman with a solar powered calculator and a watch for his wife. We gave George a waterproof watch with all the bells and whistles. They gave us brightly painted Russian dolls for Dave's daughters, some Russian chocolates, and bars of perfumed soap.

We had moved up our departure because of a threatening forecast, which could have held us hostage for days extra in Provideniya, and while the breeze was strengthening and a haze was developing the weather was holding well enough. At the airport we paid 241 dollars for landing fees and fuel. I personally refueled our plane to make doubly sure we were getting jet fuel and not gasoline and that the tanks were completely full.

Our flight plan was filed directly to Anchorage, but once we left Soviet airspace we contacted Nome and filled in the flight plan by way of Unalakleet and McGrath. Then we realized we could cut down on our over-water flying by altering course to Emmonak. A solid cloud cover obscured the coast and extended inland some fifty miles, almost to Anvik on the Yukon River. After that it was familiar country to me. It took us four hours and fifty minutes from Provideniya to Anchorage.

Dave and I were elated at having successfully completed the first private, single-engine flight from Alaska to the USSR and at having shared a little bit of glasnost with our Soviet neighbors.

25

Flying into the Sunset

The great cliché applied to bush pilots is that there are old pilots and there are bold pilots, but there are no old, bold pilots. Lowell Thomas Jr. has heard the adage many times, but when he does he begins ticking off the names of Alaska bush pilots whom he believes fit the description of being exceptions to the perception— himself included.

If it was up to Thomas he would have kept flying planes all of his life. However, the reason why pilots do eventually retire is because their reflexes slow with age, their vision dims the way other fellow senior citizens' does, and the body just isn't up to the task anymore.

By the time Thomas retired his wings he had flown at least a million miles and perhaps 1.2 million miles. He has his logbooks and they account for ten thousand hours of flying. By his calculation the average hour in the air was covered at 120 miles an hour—times ten thousand.

That doesn't mean Thomas is grounded. He and wife, Tay, still vacation in exotic places where they must take commercial jets to get around, just like the other paying passengers. He remains wedded to Tay, for more than sixty years, and he remains wedded to Alaska, home for more than fifty years.

Lowell and Tay Thomas.

With a full head of gray hair as he approached his ninetieth birthday, Thomas is not as spry and athletic as he was in his younger days, but is keenly interested in the same topics that have long captivated him, including aviation, adventure, and Alaska. While he has retired his downhill skis, Thomas seems energetic enough to tackle a cross-country ski trail for the exercise once in a while.

Later in life Thomas was also the recipient of some special awards honoring his contributions to various causes and his achievements as a pilot.

❖ ❖ ❖

LOWELL: I loved flying in the wilderness and admiring the beauty of Alaska and flying my own plane around the country and overseas and I have great memories of doing that. Making hundreds of flights to Mount McKinley with tourists was grand, but they tended to blend when everything went smoothly and we saw the same sights. I better remember the details of forced landings when things went wrong. That's probably because some unusual circumstance was encountered or some mistake was made. If something life threatening occurs you are bound to remember it because it shakes you up and you have a tendency to learn from it.

Once at Camp Denali someone had inadvertently gotten ahold of one of my drums of jet fuel that was marked Jet A. It was used by the people at the camp and they put some other stuff in it. I also had some Jet B fuel there. The Jet A fuel had been replaced by some gasoline and alcohol, some leftover stuff. When I went to use the drum it seemed to be full and it still had Jet A fuel marked on it, but there was something else in it. Well, I pumped it into the tanks of the airplane and took off with several passengers and pretty soon it just didn't work.

It was a terrible mistake—very, very serious. We are all very lucky that I landed the plane cleanly. That was the final time where I felt the Lord was on my side when I had a forced landing with a plane. That was in 1994. I got vapor lock and the engine quit. It was a pretty frantic moment all right. You don't have much time to do anything about it. I had a full load of passengers and I had to get them down. I think I had six on board. The passengers were probably a bit scared, but I didn't tell them what was going on. I was pretty busy.

I brought the plane down on a long-abandoned tundra ridge strip. Folks were flown back to Camp Denali in a helicopter summoned from Denali Park. Later, I returned with a mechanic and it was confirmed that there was a mix of fuel that produced the vapor lock in the fuel line. Had the vapor lock occurred just seconds sooner we couldn't have cleared the ridge and would have gone down on the tundra. That surely would have torn off the nose wheel and strut and it was likely the plane would have flipped on its back with serious injuries to all aboard. If the flameout happened a little bit later we would have been over the Muldrow or Traleika Glaciers and the consequences could only be imagined.

These types of things happen irregularly, but if you fly a million miles things are going to occur. Tay used to worry about me every time I took off, but she got over that and just put her faith in my ability as a pilot. She once said that I was a frustrated bush pilot for years based on the fact that it was what I wanted to do but wasn't doing it. Later, once I got going full time as a pilot and she stopped being as nervous, she said she hoped I would keep on flying until I was eighty years old. I actually surpassed that. To keep going as long as I did, flying about sixty-five years, you had to be passionate about it. But you also had to be prudent and responsible and make sure you followed your own rules very carefully at all times.

If you put the wrong fuel in an airplane, it eventually fails and that's your fault. It's always the pilot's fault, even if somebody else did the refueling. The buck stops with the pilot. I never let other people fuel my airplanes if I could help it.

The gods have been kind in teaching me how to recognize and deal with a host of aviation risks without wrecking a plane or getting hurt. How else would you explain my forced landings I've had without a scratch? I long ago came to believe that you may be allowed to make a particular mistake as a pilot once without penalty, but not the same mistake a second time.

There were always Alaska visitors who just loved to be in a small plane flying around Mount McKinley to take a look at the peak up close and to look down at the glaciers. Sometimes we could even see the climbers on the slopes, struggling to get up the mountain, but from the height we were at they almost looked like little dots. I have flown many places commercially and I don't sit there saying I wish I was flying the plane. What I wish the pilots would do is give out more information about where we are and what we're passing below. If I'm traveling with Tay I keep saying it on the plane, asking why the pilot doesn't tell us where we are. They used to be very good about it. They don't seem to care anymore. In terms of information when you're flying somewhere they should say, "Look out the window." You know, Alaska Airlines in the state has always been better than the other airlines. I've noticed that. They used to tell you, "Mount McKinley is coming up."

When I introduced myself, a lot of the flightseers knew my name. Many of them had listened to my father, but they didn't confuse me with him, though they knew his name from his broadcasts.

Between skiing, making films, writing, and especially flying, and of course having a wonderful family, I'd have to say that I did what I wanted to do with my life. It worked out very well. And I guess I am an old, bold pilot. I think if you're going to fly in Alaska you almost by definition are a bold pilot.

I started shooting with a 16-millimeter camera when I was about twelve and I kept on using that. I never got into 35-millimeter or wide-screen filming. I worked as an advance man for some outfits that were using it, but I never handled the equipment. There have been so many changes and advancements now with the digital stuff. It's just mind-boggling what's out there. The fact that you can take a good picture with a tiny little gadget that's also a telephone is pretty amazing. I was content with using older things that were still good, but I don't see the end to the technology changes coming anytime soon.

It's the same thing with airplanes. They build new airplanes, but in my mind the Cessna would still be useful and the Helio Courier and the Super Cub. There will always be a need for them. I can't see how you would make many improvements. They're good for slow flying and slow landing and very useful in very small places where you can land and take off.

I wonder if I would have been so taken with aviation if I hadn't had the chance to meet those famous early flyers and been enthralled by their stories when they visited our house. I just kept thinking, "Boy, this is the thing, and it's what I want to do if I ever get the chance."

By learning in the Air Corps I didn't have to pay to take flying lessons. Fortunately, I didn't have to go off and kill anybody through aviation. I just learned the real basics of aviation. In a small plane there is just such a feeling of freedom. You can go where you want to go and you can really see everything. It's just a wonderful feeling of total freedom. You can fly through clouds or you can climb high around a thunderhead. Flying every time is an adventure. I imagine sailing across the Atlantic would be much the same if you were in your own sailboat.

Being a pilot in Alaska kind of multiplied the adventure versus, say, being a pilot in Georgia or Louisiana. It made it much more fun, more exciting, to look at the mountains and the wildlife, and to fly over vast

A view flying over the Arctic Ocean.

empty areas. Those were not places other people could get to without an airplane. The closest thing I had to flying around Alaska was flying around Africa, the sand versus the snow. It was the same kind of adventure.

Flying over the Arctic Ocean was a great adventure too, and I did that several times. You had to be very concerned about the possibility of a forced landing if the engine quit out there. We'd land on the ice and every time I was out there the ice was still very thick. We landed on the ice with skis. I was persuaded to carry a rifle with me when I left the airplane and I did see a polar bear that got pretty close. The guys out there said, "You'd better watch out. Better be prepared, just in case." And he just showed up. A polar bear stuck his head inside the ice building we were in and there were tracks all over the area. He must have wanted to be an extra in the movie.

I heard recently that people in Kaktovik are getting involved in polar bear tourism. The theme is a sad one, though. It's of the variety of "Come see the polar bears before they're gone" as if they are saying that global warming is going to get them and wipe them out. That would be scary to lose the polar bears.

Pretty much everywhere I went in Alaska over the years I kept taking photographs and filming and for years and years I always had an illustrated lecture on Alaska going out to the lower states in the winter.

One time in the early nineties, in the spring before a tourist season began, I wanted to take a lower states trip, but Tay didn't want to go, so I took off for the Grand Canyon and ventured on to New England to visit Anne and her family. I also stopped in Pawling to visit old haunts. I just felt like flying myself on a vacation. It was a very smooth trip, but would have been more fun if Tay came along or I had other company.

My Air Force past caught up to me in 1991 with news that there was going to be a fiftieth anniversary celebration of the creation of Columbus Air Force Base in Columbus, Mississippi, and an invitation to attend. That's where I had received my wings and commission in December of 1944. I thought, "Why not fly my own plane back to Dixie for the party?" I was in the Cessna, but was grounded by thunderstorms in Dubuque, Iowa, and had to travel the rest of the way via commercial jet. Also, at that point I had not received clearance to land the plane at my old base. It had been converted into a highly active jet fighter training base. When I got there nothing was recognizable except the water tower. My old runways had given way to newer and longer ones. The many World War II wooden barracks had been replaced with permanent brick ones. Basically, only the water tower and the name were the same.

It turned out that of all the veterans who were once based there I was the one who traveled the farthest for the reunion. The next day I was taken into a booth beside the active runway to watch students shoot touch-and-goes in thundering jets. What a contrast to my days almost fifty years earlier when I instructed cadets in the plywood twin-engine piston AT-10.

In the early 1990s, board members of the National Parks Conservation Association were guests at Camp Denali and some flew with me. There was no one on the board from Alaska, which seemed something of an oversight given the many national parks in our state. They asked if I would join as Alaska's representative and "You bet!" was my response. I made annual spring trips to Washington, D.C., for the meetings.

It would have been cheaper to fly commercially, but I took myself to the meetings. One was in Bar Harbor, Maine.

I stayed on the NPCA board for six years, never contributing much I felt. To make up for that, when I went off the board I made a donation of $500,000, half going to a subsidiary—The National Park Trust. Largely as a result of my contribution, I suppose, in 1996 NPCA honored me at its annual dinner with the William Penn Mott Award as "Conservationist of the Year." The next Alaskan on the board was my friend Wally Cole and then former Alaska lieutenant governor Fran Ulmer.

Around that time I joined the board of the Alaska Conservation Foundation. This work appealed to me the same way the issues had when I was working in state government. I still believed it was important to work to protect Alaska's unique environment to the fullest during the coming years of economic development. I viewed the Alaska Conservation Foundation as the hub of a wheel, funneling funds to its spokes, each a worthy conservation entity. I added to its endowment with a large chunk of my Disney stock worth $1 million.

At one point I was asked to join the board of the Alaska Aviation Safety Foundation. Tom Wardleigh, who was an air taxi pilot for many years, was the founder. He was dedicated to improving the state's poor aviation safety record and at his request I spoke to pilots at safety seminars about flying through the mountains in a safe manner. My McKinley years offered plenty of experience to draw upon. At one seminar in Fairbanks I stressed that good judgment was the main key to safety in the air and good judgment stemmed from experiences that came out of bad judgment. I urged them to learn from the mistakes of others like mine.

Tay and I still had an interest in seeing the world's exotic places and we took a joyful cruise in the South Pacific. We flew from Los Angeles to New Zealand to Papeete and cruised from Tahiti to the Fiji Islands and to the Cook Islands. We were aboard the MS *World Discoverer* (which had an ill-fated problem later, striking an uncharted reef in the Solomon Islands). We visited Tonga and Rarotonga, where Tay's brother Tap lived and was a special assistant to the governor. There was bird life to see and side trips to see Fijian war dances with those participating wielding spears and shields. The ship was German built and one of the Zodiacs aboard bore the name Luckner painted on its side. Yes, it was named for Count Felix Von Luckner, my father's old friend, and the visitor who had regaled me with stories as a youth. The captain and I had an interesting conversation on the bridge about it.

There has always been a feeling that pilots have to retire when they reach a certain age because they have to be slowing down. Commercial airlines used to force pilots to retire at sixty and that was changed to sixty-five. I felt I could continue in a private plane, just flying myself, not customers, as long as I felt OK.

My first sign of a health problem appeared in 1994, my last year of flying commercially. I developed high blood pressure. Then I had congestive heart failure brought on by a medication. A pill solved that and the blood pressure. I also had been suffering from leg pains.

However, on that South Pacific cruise with Tay while in Papeete I suddenly blacked out mentally while crossing a street. I began to stagger and was about to fall down when a couple who had been with us on a bus caught me. It was low blood sugar. We bought some glucose at a pharmacy to reduce my chances of falling overboard. Back at home a specialist in Anchorage felt I might be suffering from a rare disease called insulinoma.

I ended up with an appointment at the Mayo Clinic that overlapped with retrieving my plane from Gardner, Massachusetts, where it had been left for a thorough inspection. At the Mayo Clinic they picked up some sort of tumor attached to my pancreas and informed me that was what likely caused the insulinoma. The doctor was shocked when I told him I had flown the plane to the clinic and was going to fly it back to Alaska. He ordered me not to do so, but relented when I told him I made it there by eating many sugary things like candy bars and cookies. He said downing sugar cubes would be better.

It's unknown how many sugar cubes I devoured on my way back to Anchorage, but when I returned to the Mayo Clinic for the surgery the next month I flew commercial with Tay. But my blood sugar problem was ancient history after the operation.

If it had been in my power I would have kept flying forever, but by 2009 it became obvious I was going to have to ground my plane. Tay wanted me to stop flying and it became a struggle to pass the FAA exam. The two things together forced me to retire and I sure do miss it. I sure as hell do. It's a way of life. I was hoping to make it to ninety, but had to retire at eighty-six. It's kind of like what a divorce might be like.

It's not fair to jeopardize everything if you don't have the proper medical clearance and something goes wrong and you're not insured. You can't get insurance if you can't pass the medical tests. I wasn't tired of flying. No, never. I'm sure I could still do the flying right now with planes I'm familiar with. You don't forget those things. I still have my eyesight and my hearing. My coordination is still pretty good, good enough. But I wouldn't want to be flying in heavy instrument weather. That would not be very wise.

Hell, it's just one of those things eventually you have to give up even though you don't want to. Tay said I should have developed other hobbies when I was in my fifties and sixties. I'm still able to drive. I feel I could still get in my airplane and get out there. I'm sure I could check it out and take off and fly in a pinch. I wish I had the opportunity. I wish someone would say, "Lowell, you'd better come down here. We really desperately need somebody to do something with this airplane. Come on and take it over to someplace." It isn't going to happen.

I donated the Helio Courier to the Alaska Aviation Museum in Anchorage. That plane was built in 1960 and it's a classic. It's not a very common airplane. There are a lot more Cessnas flying than there are Helios. I gave the Cessna to our daughter, Anne, when she earned her pilot's license. Perhaps Cessna should put me in its advertising. On the Cessna, I could say in a commercial, "I flew this plane around the world fifty-five years ago and it's still going strong." On the Helio Courier I could say, "I flew this plane for fifty years. It's a great plane." That would be funny. That would be great. That would be alright with me. Those planes do last longer than cars.

The Alaska Aviation Museum was very kind to me in 2012. They gave me a lifetime achievement award on March 22. That was pretty

Lowell standing with his Helio Courier, one of the planes he flew for decades.

nice. I was notified over the telephone and they said they were going to honor me because of all my Alaska flying, the work on the mountain, and the rescue flights. It was an honor. The recognition said I flew ten thousand hours and as I said I estimate that each hour is about 120 miles, so that would put me at something more than 1.2 million miles of flying in my life.

With military flying and private flying over the years it adds up. If a guy flies a couple of hundred hours a year it grows pretty fast. It might even be more than 1.2 million. It's a lot of miles. Thank God it was in the air and not on the road.

Going into the Alaska Aviation Museum, I was very honored. I thought it was great to be identified with people like Bob Reeve and Mudhole Smith. It was pretty neat. It wasn't anything I'd asked for, but I was very pleasantly surprised. It's nice to get those recognitions once in a while. I never did anything specifically to gain recognition, but it's a nice thing when people take note and remember you. The awards say, "Hey, you did a pretty good thing."

A Note About Sources

The vast majority of the material included in this autobiography of Lowell Thomas Jr. was taken from lengthy tape-recorded interviews about his recollections made during 2012. In addition, a small amount of material was included from prior interviews done over the years with coauthor Lew Freedman.

Some material was also compiled separately by Lowell Thomas over the years in diary format and taken from these unpublished writings. Other material was taken from reports he made in books chronicling his earlier life adventures.

In some instances, Tay Thomas, Lowell's wife of more than sixty-four years, contributed recollections from the adventures and journeys she shared with her husband before her passing in October 2014. Lowell Thomas Sr., Lowell's father, passed away in 1981. However, he was a prolific writer and in some cases his published work touched on some of the adventures he shared with his son.

Books written by Lowell Thomas Jr. that were consulted were *Out of This World: Across the Himalayas to Forbidden Tibet*. One book cowritten by Lowell Thomas Jr. and Tay Thomas consulted was *Our Flight to Adventure*. One book cowritten by Lowell Thomas Jr. and Lowell Thomas Sr. consulted was *Famous First Flights That Changed History*. Books written by Lowell Thomas Sr. consulted were *Good Evening Everybody* and *So Long Until Tomorrow*.

Index